C000064159

The Claret & Blue Book of
WEST HAM UNITED
HAMMERS HISTORY, TRIVIA, FACTS & STATS

JOHN NORTHCUTT

The Claret & Blue Book of
WEST HAM UNITED
HISTORY, TRIVIA, FACTS & STATS

All statistics, facts and figures are correct as of 20 July 2007

© John Northcutt
John Northcutt has asserted his rights in accordance with the Copyright,
Designs and Patents Act 1988 to be identified as the author of this work.

Published By:
Pitch Publishing (Brighton) Ltd
10 Beresford Court
Somerhill Road
Hove BN3 1RH

Email: info@pitchpublishing.co.uk
Web: www.pitchpublishing.co.uk

First published 2007

A catalogue record for this book is available from the British Library.

10-digit ISBN: 1-9054110-2-2
13-digit ISBN: 978-1-9054110-2-3

Printed and bound in Great Britain by CPI Group

FOREWORD BY TONY GALE

My love affair with West Ham started in the summer of 1984 when I decided that I would be leaving Fulham, the club where I started my career. Both Chelsea and West Ham were interested in signing me and had matched Fulham's transfer valuation, so it was basically left to me to decide which club I wanted to join. But after meeting with Chelsea manager John Neal and West Ham boss John Lyall there was only one winner.

In fact, my meeting with John Lyall had not even ended when my wife Lyndsey nudged me and said I should go to West Ham. Like nearly everybody who knew, played under and worked with John, she was impressed with the way he conducted himself and handled others. And so was I. John was not only my manager, he was everybody's favourite uncle. All the players knew if they had problems, either on the field or off it, they could always go to John. He was one of the main reasons my move to the club went so seamlessly.

I can still remember arriving at Chadwell Heath for my first day of training. It was a baking hot July morning, and after getting changed into our training kit, the players received the welcome news that we would be going swimming. Great, I thought, until we were told we would be running to and from the baths, some three miles away. I have to laugh when I hear managers these days talking about taking their players swimming as if it is some breathtaking new fitness development. We were doing it nearly a quarter of a century ago.

Every player who has played for West Ham retains an affection for the club, no matter where else they have plied their trade, and the ten years I spent at West Ham were amongst the happiest of my career. I don't know whether it is due to the links with nearby docks, but West Ham are, and should always be, a club for the working man. And that heritage is something that should never be forgotten in this era of executive boxes and corporate entertainment.

The club has a special place in the heart of London's East End, and the football world in general. If West Ham is not your first club, they are usually your second. Upton Park, or the Boleyn Ground to give it its proper title, has a tradition of producing entertaining football and John Lyall certainly made players aware of that in my time at the club.

Like all managers, he was never happy losing, but if we lost a thriller 4-3 he would come into the dressing-room and concede to the players: "That was great entertainment." How many bosses have an appreciation for the game like that? But that's how stylish he was. John Lyall should be rhyming slang for style, in every sense. The man oozed it and so did his teams. And none more so than his 1985/86 line-up, which I played in and recorded the club's highest-ever League finish – third in the old First Division.

After a sticky start, we recovered to mount a serious title challenge before we were hampered by fixture congestion at the end of the season. It was very harsh on us, as I firmly believe we deserved to win the Championship that year. I also think most of football wanted us to break the Merseyside domination of the title at that time.

I was lucky enough to win the Premiership title with Blackburn nine years later, but the Rovers side was not as good as that West Ham one and that 1986 heartbreak remains my biggest regret in the game. It was a season those who witnessed it will never forget, but reading through this book you realise just how much history has been created by the club that began life as Thames Ironworks in 1895.

I hope you enjoy reading the book and learning a few new things that make the club so special.

Tony Gale

INTRODUCTION

First of all I would like to thank Pitch for giving me the opportunity to write this book about my favourite club. It is not meant to be a history of the club, just a collection of trivia, statistics, facts and events that have occurred from the early days of Thames Ironworks to the club's present position in the Premier League.

The book is not set out in any particular order so you will find each page brings you a different insight into the history of West Ham United. The triumphs, the heartbreaks and the big matches are all there, culminating in a complete list of all the players who have been fortunate to wear the claret and blue shirt.

I hope that our supporters will find something of interest as they read through the book. West Ham is more than a football club – it is the heartbeat of a larger community. In these days of commercial activities, corporate advertising and sponsorship, we must not forget our proud heritage and traditions. Let's keep those bubbles flying high. After the turbulence of the previous campaign we can now look forward to an exciting season. We have an ambitious chairman, an experienced manager, and good players backed by our loyal fans.

I would like to acknowledge the help given to me by Stuart Allen on the players appearances and also Roy Shoesmith who helped on various queries.

Finally may I thank Tony Gale for writing the foreword to this book. He was a stylish defender in his playing career, making 359 appearances for West Ham, and now is a respected member of the Sky Sports team and newspaper columnist

John Northcutt

THE FORMATION OF WEST HAM UNITED

The origins of West Ham United can be traced back to the Thames Ironworks Shipbuilding Company, situated at the mouth of the River Lea at Blackwall in East London. The company had been building ships for the Royal Navy and overseas governments since it was formed in 1846. HMS Warrior, built in 1860, was at the time the biggest warship in the world. Arnold Hills, the chairman of Thames Ironworks, was instrumental in the formation of the football club. Dave Taylor, a foreman at the works, formed a football team after approaching Hills, and advertised this in the firm's gazette on 29 June 1895. A local club, Old Castle Swifts, had recently folded, and a number of their players were employed at the Ironworks. Permission was granted to use a ground in Hermit Road, Canning Town. The opening game was a home friendly against Royal Ordnance on 7 September 1895, which finished 1-1, with Arthur Darby on target. In that first season they played a series of friendly matches, and didn't enter a league – but they did enter the FA Cup, which brought a 5-0 defeat at Chatham. In 1896, they joined the London League. It was in July 1900 that the name was changed to West Ham United. These days of Premiership football, all-seater stadiums and televised games seem light years away from their humble beginnings as a works team, yet the passion is the same, with West Ham a way of life for thousands in East London and beyond.

FIRST BLACK PLAYERS

When making his West Ham debut in May 1963, John Charles became the first black player to play for the club. He was also the first black player to represent England when he gained the first of his youth caps. By the time John played his last game for the club, another black player, Clyde Best from Bermuda, was settled in the side. Next was Ade Coker from Nigeria in 1971, and he was quickly followed by Clive Charles, younger brother of John. All these players were trailblazers, and played when crowds made it difficult for them.

FA CUP SEMI-FINAL VENUES

West Ham have been involved in seven FA Cup semi-finals, played at the following grounds:

Villa Park	1975, 1980, 1991, 2006
Stamford Bridge	1923, 1975 replay
Hillsborough	1964
Elland Road	1980 replay
Molineux	1933

ANFIELD HOODOO

The last time West Ham beat Liverpool at Anfield was way back in September 1963, when goals from Hurst and Peters gave the Hammers a 2-1 win. Since then, there have been 35 league games played, and West Ham have failed to win any. They have drawn nine and lost 26. West Ham have failed to score in 24 of those matches, and have been beaten by scores of 6-0 in 1984 and 5-0 in 1998. There was also a 5-1 defeat in 1989, which condemned the Hammers to relegation to the Second Division. During this time, there have been two League Cup ties, in 1973 and 1982, which Liverpool were also victorious. So that's 37 games without a win, and it is hoped – at least in east London – that the run will not continue for much longer.

THAMES IRONWORKS' FIRST COMPETITIVE MATCH

Thames Ironworks were drawn at home to Chatham in the FA Cup in 1895/96, their first season of football. The Kent side would be formidable opponents, as they were a club of long standing and had first entered the FA Cup as long ago as 1882. Chatham protested that the Hermit Road ground was not suitable, and asked that the game be played on their ground. The Ironworks officials agreed to this, no doubt hoping that there would be extra revenue. The attendance of 3000 justified the decision. Chatham were leading 2-0 at half time, and went on to an easy victory by 5-0. The inexperienced Thames side learnt from this game, however – when the teams next met, in 1899, Chatham were beaten 4-0 in the Southern League. The Irons team for that first cup tie was: Watson, Tull, Williams, Stewart, French, Parks, Woods, Sage, Lindsay, Freeman, Darby.

WE WON THE CUP I

West Ham won the FA Cup for the first time in 1964, when they beat Preston North End 3-2 at Wembley. Doug Holden put Preston in the lead after ten minutes, but Johnny Sissons was soon to equalise. Five minutes before half-time Preston regained the lead, from a header by Alex Dawson. The Hammers were level again after 52 minutes, when Geoff Hurst headed home. There were chances for both teams before West Ham won the game in the dying seconds. Peter Brabrook put over a cross and Ronnie Boyce was on hand to head it clear of Alan Kelly. The East Londoners were on their way to a fabulous European adventure. The West Ham team was: Jim Standen, John Bond, Jack Burkett, Eddie Bovington, Ken Brown, Bobby Moore, Peter Brabrook, Ronnie Boyce, Johnny Byrne, Geoff Hurst, Johnny Sissons.

LONGEST SURNAME

When you sign a Yorkshire-born player from Barnsley, you do not expect his surname to be Otulakowski. That is what happened in 1976 when the midfielder, whose family originally came from Poland, joined West Ham from the Tykes. However, this was not the longest Hammers surname. That record is held by two players. Firstly, W. Miecznikowski, who made three appearances in 1902. He was also of Polish descent, but was born in London. The other player with 13 letters in his name was Charlie Satterthwaite, who played 32 games in 1903. More recently, in 1982, the Hammers had Dave Swindlehurst – 12 letters – in their forward line.

THAMES IRONWORKS FIRST-EVER MATCH

After forming a football team in 1895 Thames played their first game, a friendly against the reserve side of Royal Ordnance. The game took place at the Hermit Road ground on 7 September 1895. The game finished 1-1 with a first half goal from Darby. So Arthur Darby an outside left will go down in history as being the club's first-ever goalscorer. He was employed at Thames as an engineer's labourer and had previously played for local sides Old St Lukes and St Lukes.

MANAGERS

West Ham have had the fewest managers of any long-term league club. At the start of 2007/08 they had appointed only eleven in their entire history:

> Syd King.................................1902 to 1932
> Charlie Paynter.......................1932 to1950
> Ted Fenton ....1950 to 1961
> Ron Greenwood...................1961 to 1974
> John Lyall ....1974 to 1989
> Lou Macari.............................1989 to 1990
> Billy Bonds............................1990 to 1994
> Harry Redknapp ....1994 to 2001
> Glen Roeder ....2001 to 2003
> Alan Pardew ....2003 to 2006
> Alan Curbishley....................... From 2006

King, Fenton, Lyall, Bonds, Redknapp and Curbishley were all former players at the club. The year of 2006 saw the passing of Ron Greenwood in February, followed by John Lyall two months later – two great managers who will be sorely missed at Upton Park.

QUEEN'S HONOURS LIST

The following West Ham players have been honoured by the Queen:

Bobby Moore ....OBE 1967
Martin Peters............................ MBE 1978
Geoff Hurst.............................. MBE 1979
Trevor Brooking .... MBE 1981
Billy Bonds.............................. MBE 1988
Ian Wright............................... MBE 2000
Clyde Best .... MBE 2005
Dave Sexton ....OBE 2005
Teddy Sheringham .... MBE 2007

Former West Ham manager Ron Greenwood received the CBE in 1981, while Sir Geoff Hurst and Sir Trevor Brooking received knighthoods in 1998 and 2004 respectively.

SPONSORS

The first sponsors of the club were Avco Trust, who joined up for the 1984-85 season. After them came BAC Windows (1989 to 1992), Dagenham Motors (1992 to 1997), Dr Martens (1998 to 2003), and Jobserve (2003 to 2007). XL Leisure took over at the start of the 2007/08 season. Surprisingly, the club was not sponsored in the 1997/98 season.

DISMISSALS

There have been three occasions when a player has been sent off three times in the same season – Frank Piercy in 1907/08, Julian Dicks in 1992/93, and Jermain Defoe in 2003/04. Over the years, there have been eight West Ham players sent off against Leeds United, starting with Harry Redknapp in 1968. The others were Michael Hughes, Neil Ruddock, Ian Wright, Shaka Hislop, Steve Lomas, Marc Vivien Foe and Fredi Kanoute. Jeroen Boere was sent off on his debut, after coming on as a substitute at Newcastle United in September 1993. A strange occurrence came in the home match with Watford in September 1916. The Hammers winger Herbert Ashton was sent off, but before he had time to leave the field the visitors goalkeeper, Williams, intervened and won him a reprieve. Two players have had their red cards rescinded after the referee had later studied video evidence. These were Alvin Martin against Sheffield Wednesday in January 1995, and Paul Konchesky, who was red-carded against Newcastle United in August 2005. The first Hammer ever to be dismissed was Henry Hird, when playing for Thames Ironworks against Leyton in October 1897.

TELEVISION SIGNING

When Billy Dare signed for West Ham from Brentford in 1955, he became the first player to be transferred in the presence of television cameras. The transfer took place on the BBC's 'Sportsview' programme. He went on to make 119 appearances, scoring 49 goals.

UP FOR THE CUP I

Before 1967, the League Cup Final was played on a home-and-away basis. West Ham reached the final in 1966, where they lost to West Bromwich Albion over two legs. They knocked out five teams en route to the final:

Stage	Opponents	Outcome
Second round	Bristol Rovers (a)	3-3
Second round replay	Bristol Rovers (h)	3-2
Third round	Mansfield Town (h)	4-0
Fourth round	Rotherham United (a)	2-1
Quarter-final	Grimsby Town (a)	2-2
Quarter-final replay	Grimsby Town (h)	1-0
Semi-final first leg	Cardiff City (h)	5-2
Semi-final second leg	Cardiff City (a)	5-1
Final first leg	West Bromwich Albion (h)	2-1
Final second leg	West Bromwich Albion (a)	1-4

In the home leg of the final, goals from Johnny Byrne and Bobby Moore gave West Ham a 2-1 advantage, but sadly a lone goal from Byrne was not enough in the return at the Hawthorns. The Hammers team for the home leg was: Standen, Burnett, Burkett, Peters, Brown, Moore, Brabrook, Boyce, Byrne, Hurst, Dear. In the return leg, Bovington and Sissons replaced Burkett and Dear.

THINGS THEY SAID I

In 1998, Harry Redknapp wrote in his biography:

'If I have a serious falling out with the board at Upton Park that calls for my departure, I will leave this club in probably the healthiest state it's ever enjoyed. I will be leaving behind the finest squad of players in the history of West Ham.'

Harry did have a disagreement with the chairman, and did indeed leave behind a talented squad, but unfortunately without his leadership the team was relegated in 2003.

TRAINS DELAY MATCHES

When West Ham played at Chesterfield in February 1950, they did not arrive until 4.25pm due to a freight train blocking the line. Most of the spectators had gone home after getting a refund, those who stayed numbering just 3036. The dispirited Hammers lost 1-0. Back in April 1924, there were 18,000 inside Upton Park waiting for the game with Manchester City to begin – but the City team were on a train which had stopped just outside Wembley. There had been a train crash further up the line, causing the delay, and the northern party were without any means of getting in touch. Eventually, the train arrived at Euston at 4.15pm, and they were able to contact West Ham to say they were on their way. Finally, at 5 o'clock, the Manchester party arrived, and at 5.26pm the game started. Amazingly, the crowd had shown great patience during their long wait, and most of the spectators were still there, having being entertained by the Police band. The delay did not seem to upset City, as they took the lead after seven minutes. Although the Hammers equalised before half-time, it was the visitors who went on to win 2-1.

CLUB SONG

For many years, the song *I'm Forever Blowing Bubbles* has been sung at the ground. At Upton Park, the team take to the field to the tune, and a loud rendition of 'Bubbles' often inspires the team. The words to the song are:

> I'm forever blowing bubbles
> Pretty bubbles in the air
> They fly so high
> Nearly reach the sky
> Then like my dreams
> They fade and die
> Fortunes always hiding
> I've looked everywhere
> I'm forever blowing bubbles
> Pretty bubbles in the air

GOALSCORING GOALKEEPER

George Kitchen was a fine goalkeeper who played for West Ham between 1905 and 1911, making 205 appearances. On his debut against Swindon Town, he scored the only goal of the match from the penalty spot. He went on to score a further four league goals, and one in the FA Cup against Woolwich Arsenal.

THE ORIGIN OF I'M FOREVER BLOWING BUBBLES

Generations of West Ham fans have sung *I'm Forever Blowing Bubbles* on the terraces at Upton Park, but not many are aware of how it became a West Ham anthem. The song was written in 1919 in America, and became a hit on both sides of the Atlantic. The composers were James Kendis, James Brockman and Nat Vincent, who formed their names into Jaan Kenbrovin, a pseudonym named on the original sheet music. The lyrics were added by John William Kellette. How *Bubbles* came to be associated with West Ham has been the subject of many a debate over the years. The popular theory is that the singing of this song came together with the unlikely ingredients of a soap advert and a young, curly-haired footballer. In 1829, Sir John Millais painted a portrait of his grandson watching a soap bubble he had just blown through a clay pipe. The painting was exhibited at the Royal Academy. Many years later, the Pears Soap Works used the painting as an advertisement, and displayed posters throughout the East End of London. As the soap works was situated in Canning Town, the West Ham supporters would have been familiar with the posters. The West Ham Boys team often played their home games at Upton Park in front of huge crowds, and one of their team, Will Murray, having fair curly hair, resembled the boy in the advert. He soon gained the nickname "Bubbles" Murray and whenever he played the crowd would sing *I'm Forever Blowing Bubbles*, being the popular song of the day. "Bubbles" Murray became famous, and was mentioned in the programme in May 1921, when West Ham Boys played Liverpool in the English Schools Football Championship Final. Amongst the crowd of 30,000 at the Boleyn Ground that day was the Duke of York, later to become King George VI. Around that time, the Beckton Gas Works Band used to play *Bubbles* before the kick-off, and this tradition continued up until the 1970s via the Metropolitan Police Band, the Leyton Silver Band, and finally the British Legion Band. Although the song became popular all around the ground, there was particular affinity with the fans who stood in what was known as the "Chicken Run". It was an encouraging sight to the team as the supporters swayed from side to side while singing *Bubbles*. It was first believed that *Bubbles* was sung at the 1923 FA Cup final, when the Hammers met Bolton Wanderers, but this was not the case, as a souvenir leaflet issued on the day had words to be sung by the Hammers fans to the tune of Till We Meet Again. Another theory about the origins of *Bubbles* concerned the connection with Swansea Town (now Swansea City). Between 1920 and 1926, the Welsh fans used to sing *Bubbles* at their home games, and this was mentioned in the history of Swansea Town, published in 1982. There was a close affinity between the two clubs. The old grounds were similar, and the areas surrounding them were industrial and working class, and each could identify with the other. Various Swansea match reports mentioned the singing. A report for the home game with Bury in 1921 mentioned 'the ever-popular singing of *Bubbles* from the main bank with a tremendous sway'. For the cup-tie with Clapton Orient in 1924, it was stated that once again the crowd swayed to *Bubbles*. The "Leader" in 1925 reported on the Swans trip to Southend United, saying 'the support was considerable, with lusty renderings of *Bubbles*'. Finally the report for the FA Cup tie with Aston Villa in 1925 said that 'despite the rendering of *Cwm Rhondda* and *Bubbles* the Villa won 3-1'. In 1922, West Ham played Swansea Town three times in the FA Cup, with a game at both grounds and a replay at Ashton Gate in Bristol. It could be, therefore, that the Hammers supporters adopted the song after this. In those days of friendly rivalry, it was possible that both sets of supporters would have sung *Bubbles* and swayed to join in the fun. The author Brian Belton, in doing research for his various West Ham books, has put forward another interesting theory. During World War II, *Bubbles* was sung as crowds gathered during air raids in shelters and underground stations, especially in blitz-torn East London. This led to a rise in communal singing, both in the Forces and the general public, to raise morale. This could explain how *Bubbles* became the song of East End football. The song was heard at the 1940 War League Cup Final, and this may mark the real beginning of it being the West Ham theme. It has endured through the years to echo the hopes and disappointment of the West Ham faithful. It has been said that the words are too sentimental for a football song, but tradition dies hard, and the Hammers supporters would not be the same without their beloved anthem. Not only is it heard at football grounds, but whenever Hammers fans get together at family gatherings and parties, they request that the tune is played. Readers may like to know that a booklet titled The "Bubbles" Legend is currently on sale at the West Ham club shop. It was written by Graham Murray, the son of Bubbles Murray. A soap advert, a curly-haired footballer, a popular song, the Swansea connection and war time community singing…the evidence behind the legend probably lies somewhere in the mists of time. One other club that has *Bubbles* as its signature tune is AFC Telford, who have used the song for many years, going back to their days as Wellington Town. Back in 1990, the players approached the club chairman, asking for a tune which would be more in keeping with the club's tradition. Through the media of the "Shropshire Star", the fans were asked what they would like, and the older supporters indicated they would like to keep *Bubbles*, with the younger fans requesting a new song. A compromise was reached when West Ham sent them a more modern version of *Bubbles*, which was recorded by the 1975 FA Cup Final squad.

STAN EARLE

Inside forward Stan Earle first joined Arsenal in 1923, where he scored on his debut against Preston North End. After only seven appearances in a Gunners shirt, he moved to West Ham in August 1924. Strangely enough, it was against Preston that he made his Hammers debut. He did not score that day, but got the winner the following week in a 1-0 victory at Blackburn Rovers. For the next seven seasons, Stan was a regular in the side, both scoring and creating chances for Vic Watson. The pair had a great season in 1926/27, when between them they scored 47 league goals. That year, Stan gained his solitary England cap, against Northern Ireland in Belfast. After playing in 273 games for West Ham, he joined Clapton Orient in 1932, where he finished his playing career after making 16 appearances. On retiring from playing, he coached Walthamstow Avenue and managed Leyton. Stan died in Brightlingsea, Essex in September 1971.

MEMORIES OF THE 1966/67 SEASON

August: For the first home game against Chelsea, the World Cup trio of Moore, Hurst, and Peters came out to a rousing reception from the crowd, who appreciated their efforts during the summer. The sudden death of Bill Jenkins was recorded. He'd been the first-team physio since 1961. Tommy Yews, a winger who made 361 appearances in the 1920s, also passed away.
September: Tottenham Hotspur were the visitors in the League Cup, their very first game in the competition. Geoff Hurst scored in the Hammers 1-0 victory.
November: Bexley United Colts were beaten 5-1 in the London Youth Cup. Future stars in the line-up included Trevor Brooking, who scored twice, and Frank Lampard (Snr). A trip to Egypt saw West Ham beaten 5-1 by Zamalek, with many of the players suffering from upset stomachs. *February:* The Hammers record a 2-0 home win against Kilmarnock in a friendly. In goal for the Scots was Bobby Ferguson, who later joined the Hammers for £65,000, then a British record fee for a goalkeeper. *March:* West Ham played at Coventry City for the Sir Winston Churchill Trophy. Goals from Brabrook (2) and Hurst saw the Hammers to a 3-3 draw. The resultant penalty shoot-out ended in a 9-7 West Ham victory.

COUSINS

Three members of the famous Allen clan all played for West Ham. First was Paul Allen, who joined in 1979 and moved to Tottenham Hotspur after making 152 league appearances. Next was Martin Allen, who signed for the club in 1989. He played in 190 league games before joining Portsmouth. Lastly, there was Clive Allen, who signed in 1991. He joined Millwall after playing in 38 league games.

ENGLAND INTERNATIONALS

The following players have represented England as West Ham players:

Player	Caps	Season
Jim Barrett	1	1928-29
Trevor Brooking	47	1973-82
Billy Brown	1	1923-24
Ken Brown	1	1959-60
Johnny Byrne	10	1962-66
Michael Carrick	2	2000-02
Joe Cole	10	2000-03
Tony Cottee	3	1986-88
Alan Devonshire	8	1979-84
Stan Earle	1	1927-28
Rio Ferdinand	10	1997-01
Paul Goddard	1	1981-82
Len Goulden	14	1936-39
Ted Hufton	6	1923-29
Geoff Hurst	49	1965-72
David James	17	2001-04
Paul Konchesky	1	2005-06
Frank Lampard snr	2	1972-80
Frank Lampard jnr	2	1999-01
Alvin Martin	17	1980-87
Billy Moore	1	1922-23
Bobby Moore	108	1961-74
John Morton	1	1937-38
Stuart Pearce	2	1999-00
Martin Peters	33	1965-70
Jimmy Ruffell	6	1925-30
Trevor Sinclair	11	2001-03
Jack Tresadern	2	1922-23
Vic Watson	5	1922-30
George Webb	2	1910-11
Ian Wright	2	1998-99

PLAYED IN OTHER COMPETITIONS

There have been three players who have played in a first-team competitive game for the club, but never got to make a league appearance. Fred Wallbanks played in the FA Cup in 1935 against Stockport County, Ralph Milne was selected against Derby County in the League Cup in 1989, and finally Rob Jones turned out against Jokerit in the Intertoto Cup in 1999.

HAMMER OF THE YEAR

Each season, the supporters vote for their choice of player to be named as Hammer of the Year. The winners have been:

1958	Andy Malcolm
1959	Ken Brown
1960	Malcolm Musgrove
1961	Bobby Moore
1962	Lawrie Leslie
1963	Bobby Moore
1964	Johnny Byrne
1965	Martin Peters
1966	Geoff Hurst
1967	Geoff Hurst
1968	Bobby Moore
1969	Geoff Hurst
1970	Bobby Moore
1971	Billy Bonds
1972	Trevor Brooking
1973	Bryan Robson
1974	Billy Bonds
1975	Billy Bonds
1976	Trevor Brooking
1977	Trevor Brooking
1978	Trevor Brooking
1979	Alan Devonshire
1980	Alvin Martin
1981	Phil Parkes
1982	Alvin Martin
1983	Alvin Martin
1984	Trevor Brooking
1985	Paul Allen
1986	Tony Cottee
1987	Billy Bonds
1988	Stewart Robson
1989	Paul Ince
1990	Julian Dicks
1991	Ludek Miklosko
1992	Julian Dicks
1993	Steve Potts
1994	Trevor Morley
1995	Steve Potts
1996	Julian Dicks

1997	Julian Dicks
1998	Rio Ferdinand
1999	Shaka Hislop
2000	Paolo Di Canio
2001	Stuart Pearce
2002	Seb Schemmel
2003	Joe Cole
2004	Matthew Etherington
2005	Teddy Sheringham
2006	Danny Gabbidon
2007	Carlos Tevez

JOE COCKROFT

Joe Cockroft was a consistent wing-half who was ever-present for four consecutive seasons. A Yorkshireman, Joe came to West Ham in 1932 from the Midland League side Gainsborough Trinity. Making his debut against Chesterfield in April 1933, he played in six games that season, and was then ever-present until March 1938, having played in an amazing 208 consecutive league games. Joe played in the side that beat Blackburn Rovers at Wembley in 1940 to win the War Cup. During the war, he guested for Sheffield Wednesday, and when hostilities ended he joined them on a permanent basis. He became club captain, and played in 97 matches before joining neighbours Sheffield United in November 1948. He had a brief spell at Bramall Lane, making 14 appearances before becoming player-manager at Wisbech Town. Joe died at the age of 82 in February 1994.

HOME OF THE HAMMERS

Since 1904, the club has played its home games at the Boleyn Ground, commonly called Upton Park. They moved there from the Memorial Grounds. At that time, the ground was a piece of rough land, and was the home of Boleyn Castle FC. There was a small grandstand on the west side, and some covered terracing backing onto Priory Road. A directors box stood in the south-west corner, and the dressing rooms were on the north-west corner beside the North Bank. The first home game was on 1 September 1904, when the Hammers beat Millwall 3-0. Since then, the stadium has been transformed into the all-seater arena it is today.

THE LONE SCOT

West Ham won the FA Cup in 1964, 1975 and 1980 using a total of 30 players in those Finals. There were 29 Englishman, the odd one out being Scottish full-back Ray Stewart, who played in 1980.

FASTEST GOAL

The quickest goal scored at Upton Park is credited to Ken Bainbridge. The goal came after 11 seconds in the game with Barnsley on 29 August 1949, and West Ham went on to win 2-1. At Nottingham Forest in May 1989, Leroy Rosenior scored after 17 seconds.

SHORT CAREER

The following players all appeared in the first team – but not for long:

Lee Boylan	1 minute v Sheffield Wednesday	May 1997
Paul Marquis	4 minutes v Manchester City	February 1994
Paul Mitchell	6 minutes v Blackburn Rovers	April 1994
Chris Coyne	7 minutes v Leeds United	May 1999
Gavin Holligan	23 minutes v Liverpool	February 1999
Mark Watson	23 minutes v Queens Park Rangers	April 1996
Mauricio Taricco	27 minutes v Millwall	November 2004
Ray Houghton	35 minutes v Arsenal	May 1982
Paul Kelly	44 minutes v Hull City	January 1990

DENIED THE CHAMPIONSHIP

On the final day of the season in 1991, the game with Notts County had ended at Upton Park, and West Ham had finished the season with 87 points. If Oldham Athletic failed to beat Sheffield Wednesday at Boundary Park, West Ham were champions. To the delight of thousands on the pitch at Upton Park, they were informed that Oldham were only drawing in injury time. The celebrating crowd were stunned into silence when they heard that Oldham had scored with a last-minute penalty. The Hammers were denied the title by one point.

MOST MATCHES IN A SEASON

The highest number of competitive games played by West Ham in a single season is 62 in 1965/66. The Hammers played 42 League games, four FA Cup matches, ten League Cup ties, and six games in the European Cup Winners Cup.

RAPID SCORING

Brian Dear scored five goals in a 20-minute spell on Good Friday April 1965, against West Bromwich Albion at Upton Park. The luckless Baggies were beaten 6-1 in a First Division match.

LEADS LOST

On six occasions, West Ham have been leading 3-0, only to fail to win. Three matches were lost and three drawn, with Stoke and West Brom involved twice. They drew 3-3 against Albion in 1961, Stoke in 1969, and Southampton in 1971. Defeats by 4-3 came against Stoke in 1967, Wimbledon in 1998, and West Brom in 2003.

FIRST-EVER LEAGUE CUP TIE

West Ham kicked off in the new competition on 26 September 1960, when a sparse crowd of 12,496 at Upton Park saw them beat Charlton Athletic 3-1. The Hammers' first goal went to Johnny Dick, followed by goals from Malcolm Musgrove and Bobby Moore. The team in that inaugural match was: Brian Rhodes, John Bond, John Lyall, Andy Malcolm, Ken Brown, Bobby Moore, Andy Smillie, Phil Woosnam, Dave Dunmore, John Dick, Malcolm Musgrove. West Ham were beaten 3-2 by Fourth Division Darlington in the next round.

PFA AWARDS

1964 .... Bobby Moore...................... Footballer of the Year
1975 .... Mervyn Day....................Young Player of the Year
1986 .... Tony Cottee....................Young Player of the Year

SCORE DRAW THRILLERS

On three occasions, West Ham have drawn 5-5 in a league game. The first was at Upton Park in January 1931 against Aston Villa, with goals from Viv Gibbins (2), Jim Harris, Jim Barrett and Tommy Yews. In December 1960, the opponents were Newcastle United at St James' Park, where the Hammers were leading 5-2 with 11 minutes remaining! The five goals were scored by John Bond, Johnny Dick, Dave Dunmore, Malcolm Musgrove, and an own goal from Alf McMichael. The final game was in December 1966 at Chelsea. Again West Ham were leading, this time by 5-3, only to see Chelsea equalise in the last minute. The Hammers goalscorers were Johnny Sissons (2), Peter Brabrook, Johnny Byrne, and Martin Peters.

OLDEST PLAYER

On 30th April 1988 Billy Bonds was 41 years 225 days old when he played against Southampton at the Dell. Prior to this, Charlie Bicknell was 41 years and 59 days old when he played his final match for the club, against Leicester City on 4 January 1947.

THE MEN IN BLACK

These are the referees who have been in charge at the FA Cup Finals:

1923 v Bolton Wanderers ....D. Asson
1964 v Preston North End.......A. Holland
1975 v Fulham.........................P. Partridge
1980 v Arsenal ....G. Courtney
2006 v Liverpool..........................A. Wiley

GROUND HISTORY

South Bank, now known as the Bobby Moore Stand: The South Bank terrace used to house the away supporters until it was demolished during the 1993/94 season to make way for the new two-tier all-seater stand. It was renamed after the club's legendary captain Bobby Moore, who sadly died in 1993. In 1944, a flying bomb fell on the stand, causing extensive damage and forcing West Ham to play a number of home games on opponents' grounds.

North Bank, now known as the Centenary Stand: For many years, this was just open terracing, but in 1961 a roof was added, which meant the ground was now covered on all sides. On 13 February 1995, the new Centenary Stand was opened. The vast majority of the supporters there are 'Family' members, but there is an area in the north-east corner which houses the away fans.

East Terrace, now known as the East Stand: For decades, this part of the ground was affectionately known as the 'Chicken Run'. It had a corrugated iron roof and a simple wooden structure. There was a unique atmosphere, as the fans used to sway as they sang a rendition of *Bubbles*. In January 1969, the terraces were replaced by a new East Stand. This was originally split between seating and standing accommodation, but is now all-seater. This stand is scheduled to be replaced soon in the final redevelopment phase of the ground.

West Stand, now known as the Dr Martens Stand: In 1913, a new, improved West Stand was built, only to be replaced in 1925 with a more substantial structure. This had seating blocks, a directors box and press facilities. It was extended in 1965, with a new section added to the south corner. The magnificent Dr Martens Stand replaced the West Stand in May 2001. The stand now includes a museum, a megastore, and 70 executive boxes that convert to hotel rooms. In May 2002, the stand was officially opened by Her Majesty The Queen.

OTHER GAMES STAGED AT UPTON PARK

FA Amateur Cup Finals
Ilford v Bournemouth 1930
Dulwich Hamlet v Marine 1932
Dulwich Hamlet v Leyton 1934
Casuals v Ilford 1936
Dulwich Hamlet v Leyton 1937

FA Vase Final
Sudbury v Brigg 2003

FA Trophy Final
Grays v Woking 2006

England Full International
v Australia 2003

England Under 21 internationals
v Poland 1982
v Bulgaria 1998
v Croatia 2003

England Under 20 international
v Switzerland 2002

England Youth Internationals
v Belgium 1948
v Luxembourg 1957
v Belgium 1969

TELEVISION

West Ham first appeared on BBC's 'Match of the Day' on 12 September 1964, when they beat Tottenham Hotspur 3-2 thanks to a Johnny Byrne hat-trick. The first game transmitted in colour was the game at Anfield on 15 November 1969, when the Hammers were beaten 2-0 by Liverpool.

THEIR NAMES BEGAN WITH B

Between 1963 and 1966 West Ham fielded 12 players whose surnames began with the letter B: Peter Bennett, Dave Bickles, Jimmy Bloomfield, John Bond, Eddie Bovington, Ronnie Boyce, Peter Brabrook, Martin Britt, Ken Brown, Jack Burkett, Dennis Burnett, Johnny Byrne.

ONE-HUNDRED-PLUS LEAGUE GOALS

The following players have scored over 100 league goals for West Ham:

Vic Watson	298
Geoff Hurst	180
Jimmy Ruffell	159
Johnny Dick	153
Tony Cottee	115

ACTION REPLAY I

7 March 1927 .... West Ham 7 Arsenal 0 .... First Division

After two minutes, the Hammers went ahead with a goal by Vic Watson from a cross by Ruffell. A quarter of an hour later it was 2-0, a shot from Watson being turned past his own goalkeeper by Parker. Shortly afterwards, Lewis failed to hold a shot from Ruffell, and Watson tapped home the third, and just before half-time there was a second own goal, when Bob John, the Gunners left-back, deflected the ball past Lewis. Soon after the restart, inside left Johnson made it 5-0. Watson claimed his hat-trick from another pass from Ruffell, and the rout was complete when Jimmy Ruffell scored the seventh goal in the last minute. The Hammers finished sixth that season, and were London's top side. The West Ham team: David Baillie, Jack Hebden, George Horler, Jimmy Collins, Jim Barrett, Albert Cadwell, Tommy Yews, Stan Earle, Vic Watson, Bill Johnson, Jimmy Ruffell.

FIRST EVER EUROPEAN COMPETITIVE GAME

West Ham travelled to Ghent in Belgium in September 1964 to play La Gantoise in the European Cup Winners Cup. A goal from Ronnie Boyce gave them a 1-0 victory. It proved to be a successful campaign, as the Hammers eventually won the trophy, beating TSV Munich in the final. The West Ham team that played in that first match was: Jim Standen, John Bond, Martin Peters, Eddie Bovington, Ken Brown, Bobby Moore, Alan Sealey, Ronnie Boyce, Johnny Byrne, Geoff Hurst, John Sissons.

CHARITY SHIELD

1964	2-2 v Liverpool *		Anfield
1975	0-2 v Derby County		Wembley
1980	0-1 v Liverpool		Wembley

* The clubs shared the shield

TOP TEN RECORD APPEARANCES

Billy Bonds 663
Frank Lampard Snr 551
Bobby Moore 544
Trevor Brooking 528
Jimmy Ruffell 505
Alvin Martin 469
Vic Watson 462
Jim Barrett 442
Geoff Hurst 411
Steve Potts 399

WE WON THE WORLD CUP

All Hammers supporters look back to 1966 and like to tell other fans that it was West Ham who won the World Cup in 1966. It was England, of course, but our three lads certainly played a big part. Geoff Hurst scored a hat-trick, and Martin Peters scored the other goal. Bobby Moore did a splendid job as captain, and picked up his third major trophy at Wembley in three years.

FLOODLIGHT OPENER

The first game played under floodlights at Upton Park was a friendly with Tottenham Hotspur on 16 April 1953. Goals from Dixon and Barrett gave the Hammers a 2-1 win before a crowd of 25,000. Playing for West Ham that night were: Ernie Gregory, George Wright, Harry Kinsell, Malcolm Allison, Doug Bing, Tommy Southren, Jim Barrett, Tommy Dixon, Jimmy Andrews, and Harry Hooper. It was said at the time that the system employed at Upton Park was better than any in Great Britain. There were no shadows or blind spots to fool players or watchers. A final touch came when the Hammers team took the field in bright fluorescent shirts.

STRANGE LEAGUE DEBUT I

West Ham were playing Arsenal at Highbury in September 1995. In those days, only three substitutes were named. Late in the second half, two of these had already been used, which left goalkeeper Les Sealey on the bench. In the 83rd minute, John Moncur left the field concussed. This meant that a bemused Sealey came on for his Hammers league debut – at centre-forward. Les finally made his debut in goal later on in the season at Newcastle.

SUBSTITUTES

West Ham's first ever used substitute was Peter Bennett, who replaced Jack Burkett in the match with Leeds United on 28 August 1965. The players who have made the most substitute appearances for West Ham United in league games, up until the end of the 2006/07 season, are as follows:

John Moncur.. 44
Bobby Zamora 43
Steve Potts 37
Don Hutchison 32
Kevin Keen.. 32
Jermain Defoe 31

The first West Ham substitute to score a goal was Pat Holland, in the FA Cup in January 1974 against Hereford United. In May 1992, Frank McAvennie came on in the second half against Nottingham Forest... and scored a hat-trick. The first game in which two substitutes were used was against Queens Park Rangers in August 1987, when Alan Dickens and Gary Strodder came on. Three substitutes were used for the first time in September 1995, when Stan Lazaridis, Alvin Martin, and Les Sealey played against Arsenal. The first Hammers substitute to be substituted was Stan Lazaridis, who was replaced by Keith Rowland in the FA Cup tie with Grimsby Town in February 1996. Other first substitutes for the club have been Ronnie Boyce in the FA Cup at Mansfield Town in February 1969, and Harry Redknapp in the League Cup at Huddersfield Town in November 1967. Keith Peacock, who was Alan Curbishley's assistant for a brief period during the 2006/07 season, was the Football League's first-ever substitute: he made history while playing for Charlton Athletic in August 1965. The first West Ham substitute to be sent off was Marco Boogers at Manchester United in August 1995.

GAME BEHIND CLOSED DOORS

In season 1980/81, West Ham were drawn to play Castilla from Spain – Real Madrid's reserve side – in the European Cup Winners Cup. In the first leg in Spain, West Ham lost 3-1, and crowd trouble followed. This resulted in UEFA decreeing that the home leg must be played behind closed doors. In an eerie atmosphere, West Ham won 5-1 and progressed to the next round. The official attendance was given as 262. This included the players, match officials, administration staff, and the watching media.

BROTHERS

Over the years there have been seven sets of brothers who have played first-team football for West Ham. George Hilsdon was a fine goalscorer who had two spells with the club, scoring 35 goals in 92 appearances between 1904 and 1914. In between he scored 107 goals in 194 appearances for Chelsea. On his debut for the Blues, he scored five goals against Glossop. Jack Hilsdon was his older brother, and came to West Ham from Clapton Orient, where he had scored more than 50 goals. With the Hammers, he only managed a solitary appearance, against Luton Town in 1903. Albert Denyer was a fine forward who, between 1912 and 1914, scored 16 goals in his 46 Southern League appearances. He later joined Swindon Town, where he had a good career, playing in 324 league games and scoring 49 goals. His brother Frank Denyer was a defender who played in two league games for the Hammers in season 1913/14. Wing-half David Corbett played four games for West Ham in 1936/37, before joining Southport. His younger brother Norman played from 1937 until 1949, making 173 appearances. A third brother, Willie, guested for West Ham during the Second World War. Benny Fenton played 22 games for the Hammers, scoring nine goals between 1937 and 1939. He went on to play for Millwall, Colchester United, and Charlton Athletic, and later managed each of them. Ted Fenton, his older brother, was West Ham manager when the club won the Second Division Championship in 1958. Ted was a player with the Hammers from 1933 until 1946, turning out 176 times. Ted and Benny played together in the same team on four occasions, and were the only brothers to do so. Bill Nelson made two appearances in 1954 before joining Queens Park Rangers. Younger brother Andy Nelson was part of the West Ham Second Division Championship squad in 1958. He played in 17 games in the late 1950s. The next set of brothers to play for the club were John and Clive Charles. John was the captain of the FA Youth Cup-winning side in 1963. A tenacious full-back, he made 142 appearances for West Ham. Clive Charles, the younger of the pair, was also a full-back. He played 15 times for the Hammers, before joining Cardiff City in 1973. Rio and Anton Ferdinand are the most recent pair. Rio played for five seasons before joining Leeds United for £18m in 2000. He played in a total of 160 league and cup games, and is now an established England international, with Manchester United. Younger brother Anton is currently at West Ham. Like Rio, he's a defender too.

DOUBLE HAT-TRICKS

There have been two instances of a player scoring six goals in a match. Vic Watson scored six against Leeds United on 9 February 1929 in an 8-2 win, while Geoff Hurst scored six when the Hammers beat Sunderland 8-0 on 19 October 1968.

RESERVE TEAM JOTTINGS

High-scoring reserve games have included a 13-2 win against Fulham in 1928, a 12-1 away victory in 1931 at Clapton Orient, and an 11-0 away defeat against Crystal Palace in 1991. An amazing crowd of 31,000 turned up on the evening of 29 April 1937, when the Hammers were at home to Arsenal. Both teams had 66 points going into the game, and the winners would be crowned champions of the London Combination. It was Arsenal who scored the only goal of the game. The first reserve game to be played under floodlights at Upton Park was the match against Fulham on 7 September 1953. West Ham must have enjoyed the experience, as they won 9-1.

LEAGUE STATUS

1898/99	Southern League Second Division
1899/1900-1914/15	Southern League First Division
1915/16-1918/19	Wartime League
1919/20-1922/23	Second Division
1923/24-1931/32	First Division
1932/33-1938/39	Second Division
1939/40-1945/46	Wartime Regional League
1946/47-1957/58	Second Division
1958/59-1977/78	First Division
1978/79-1980/81	Second Division
1981/82-1988/89	First Division
1989/90-1990/91	Second Division
1991/92	First Division
1992/93	New Division One
1993/94-2002/03	Premiership
2003/04-2004/05	The Championship
2005/06-	Premiership

STRANGE LEAGUE DEBUT II

Stan Burton played for Wolverhampton Wanderers in the FA Cup Final against Portsmouth on 29 April 1939. Within days, he signed for West Ham and made his league debut on 6 May against Manchester City in a delayed league game. This was to be his only appearance for the club.

THE AGE OF STEAM

One of a batch of 25 locomotives named after football clubs, Locomotive No 61672, 'West Ham United', entered service in July 1937 and was scrapped in March 1960. The number plate is on display at Upton Park.

TESTIMONIALS SINCE 1958

Date	Player	Opposition
17 November 1958	Malcolm Allison	All Star XI
10 October 1960	Ernie Gregory	LDA Alajeulense
27 April 1964	John Lyall	All Star XI
11 May 1966	John Bond	Ex Hammers
15 May 1967	Ken Brown	Select XI
16 November 1970	Bobby Moore	Celtic
23 November 1971	Geoff Hurst	European XI
13 November 1972	Ronnie Boyce	Manchester United
4 April 1973	Paul Heffer	Israel XI
2 November 1976	Frank Lampard Snr	Fulham
31 October 1977	Trevor Brooking	England XI
4 December 1978	Billy Bonds*	Tottenham Hotspur
13 April 1981	Bobby Ferguson	Southampton
18 May 1984	Pat Holland	Tottenham Hotspur
12 May 1986	Gerhard Ampofo	Tottenham Hotspur
9 August 1987	Eddie Chapman	Terry Venables XI
10 May 1988	Geoff Pike	Dinamo Zagreb
21 August 1988	Alvin Martin*	Tottenham Hotspur
13 August 1989	Alan Devonshire	Crystal Palace
19 August 1990	Phil Parkes	Ipswich Town
12 November 1990	Billy Bonds*	Tottenham Hotspur
13 May 1991	Paul Hilton	Crystal Palace
8 May 1994	Tony Gale	Eire XI
22 May 1995	George Parris	Ipswich Town
11 November 1995	Alvin Martin*	Chelsea
2 August 1997	Steve Potts	Queens Park Rangers
13 August 2000	Julian Dicks	Athletic Bilbao

* Both Billy Bonds and Alvin Martin were awarded two testimonials

FIRST-EVER SOUTHERN LEAGUE GAME AS WEST HAM UNITED

This took place on 1 September 1900, when West Ham hosted Gravesend United at the Memorial Ground. Within five minutes, Billy Grassam opened the scoring for West Ham, but the main danger to Gravesend came from the Hammers wingers, Hunt and Fenton. It was Fenton who crossed for Hunt to score the second, and just before half time, Reid scored the third. Almost from the restart, Hunt set up Grassam for goal number four. Reid then made it five, and two more from Grassam completed the scoring. The West Ham team for this opening game was Monteith, Tranter, Craig, Dove, Raisbeck, MacEachrane Hunt, Grassam, Reid, Kaye, Fenton.

EVER PRESENT

The best season for players being ever-present was 1958/59, when five players played in every game. These were John Bond, Ken Brown, Noel Cantwell, Mike Grice and Andy Malcolm. Johnny Dick missed only one game, and Malcolm Musgrove played all but two. This level of stability no doubt helped, as they finished sixth in Division One that season.

SCORING DEBUTANTS

Three players have managed three goals on their debut, but five can claim to have scored hat-tricks. Arthur Winterhalder v Tottenham Hotspur, on 29 December 1906; Tudor Martin v Newcastle United, on 9 September 1936; and Ken Tucker v Chesterfield, on 4 October 1947 each managed three goals on their first outing for West Ham. However, two players went one better, and scored four goals on debut: Billy Grassam v Gravesend United, on 1 September 1900; and Don Travis v Plymouth Argyle, on 16 February 1946. The last ten West Ham players to score on their first-team debut are as follows:

Kepo Blanco ....v Liverpool, 31 January 2007
Carlton Cole...............................v Charlton Athletic, 19 August 2006
David Bellion .... v Sheffield Wednesday, 20 September 2005
Bobby Zamora ....v Bradford City, 7 February 2004
John Harley.................................v Sheffield United, 17 January 2004
David Connolly.......................... v Preston North End, 9 August 2003
Jermain Defoe...v Walsall, 19 September 2000
Fredi Kanoute.. v Wimbledon, 26 March 2000
Ian Wright.............................. v Sheffield Wednesday, 15 August 1998
Trevor Sinclair .... v Everton, 31 January 1998

WARTIME WINS

During the Second World War, West Ham played in regional football, and notched up some impressive victories:

30 March 1940 ....10-3 v Chelsea
26 October 1940...............................11-0 v Southend United
12 April 1941 ....8-1 v Clapton Orient
6 September 1941 ....8-4 v Chelsea
27 September 1941 ....8-0 v Watford
2 January 1943.....................................10-3 v Clapton Orient
20 January 1945..8-1 v Aldershot
12 May 1945...9-1 v Luton Town

SCOTTISH IMPORTS

Ten players who signed for West Ham from Scottish clubs:

Allen McKnight	Celtic	1988
Tommy McQueen	Aberdeen	1986
Frank McAvennie	St Mirren	1985
Sandy Clark	Airdrie	1982
Neil Orr	Morton	1981
Ray Stewart	Dundee United	1979
Bobby Ferguson	Kilmarnock	1967
John Cushley	Celtic	1967
Ian Crawford	Heart of Midlothian	1961
Jimmy Andrews	Dundee	1951

BOBBY MOORE'S LAST GAME FOR WEST HAM

It would have been fitting if it had been played to a packed audience at Upton Park, or at a Wembley Cup final. Instead his last match for the club was before a couple of thousand fans, in a reserve game against Plymouth Argyle on 9 March 1974. What a shame that the greatest player in West Ham's history had to bow out in this fashion.

JOTTINGS FROM THE 1970s

November 1971: Two European legends play in Geoff Hurst's Testimonial at Upton Park. Playing for the European XI were Eusebio from Portugal and West Germany's Uwe Seeler. August 1972: Arsenal were awarded a penalty against West Ham at Highbury after 40 seconds. It was reported as being the fastest penalty on record. Alan Ball scored for the Gunners. January 1973: Former centre-half Ken Brown senior, while with Bournemouth, broke his leg. He was not playing at the time – he was in the coach that crashed on the way back from a game at Scunthorpe. September 1974: The Hammers go goal-crazy, scoring 20 times in eight days. In the League, there were wins over Leicester City (6-2), Birmingham City (3-0), and Burnley (5-3). In the League Cup, there's a 6-0 win against Tranmere Rovers.

FIRST BRITISH ISLES INTERNATIONALS

England	George Webb v Wales	1911
Scotland	John Dick v England	1959
Wales	William Jones v England	1902
Eire	Charlie Turner v Norway	1937
Northern Ireland	Bertie Lutton v Cyprus	1973

FATHER AND SON

Centre-half Jim Barrett played for the Hammers between 1924 and 1938, making 467 league and cup appearances. His son Jimmy was with the club from 1949 until 1954, playing in 87 games before being transferred to Nottingham Forest. Popular centre-half Ken Brown was with the club from 1952 until 1966. He won winners' medals in the 1964 FA Cup Final and the 1965 European Cup Winners Cup Final, scoring four times in 455 league and cup games. Kenny Brown junior joined West Ham in 1991 from Plymouth Argyle. He was a full-back, and made 75 appearances for the Hammers before joining Birmingham City in 1996. Bill Lansdowne senior played in the team that won the Second Division Championship in 1957/58. He made 60 league and cup appearances before becoming a coach to the club's youth team. Billy Lansdowne was with the Hammers from 1978 until 1980, when he joined Charlton Athletic. In that time, he made 14 senior appearances and scored four goals. Finally, Frank Lampard senior made a total of 663 appearances and played in two winning FA Cup Finals, in 1975 and 1980. His son, Frank junior, is now one of the best midfielders in the world. While at West Ham, he played in 185 league and cup games, scoring 37 goals, before joining Chelsea in 2001.

THE BRITISH ISLES' MOST CAPPED HAMMERS

108	Bobby Moore	England
27	Steve Lomas	Northern Ireland
17	Noel Cantwell	Eire
14	Phil Woosnam	Wales
10	Ray Stewart	Scotland

RECORD FA YOUTH CUP WIN

West Ham hold the aggregate record for an FA Youth Cup final win, beating Coventry City 9-0 over two legs in 1999. The Hammers biggest win in this competition came in 1990, when they beat Horndean from Hampshire 21-1. The game was played on Guy Fawkes night. There were certainly some fireworks that evening.

CONSECUTIVE APPEARANCES

Full-back Joe Cockroft played in an amazing 208 consecutive league games from 8 April 1933 until 26 March 1938. He was ever-present over four seasons. Goalkeeper Ludek Miklosko went closest to breaking the record, playing in a total of 162 successive league games from 11 March 1991 until 23 December 1995. He was ever-present for three seasons.

NEAR NEIGHBOURS

They may be fierce rivals, but it didn't stop these players from playing for West Ham and Spurs: Jimmy Greaves, Martin Peters, Jimmy Neighbour, Chris Hughton, Steve Walford, Paul Allen, Mitchell Thomas, Mattie Etherington, Bobby Zamora, Fredi Kanoute, Michael Carrick, Jermain Defoe, Mauricio Taricco, Ilie Dumitrescu, Les Ferdinand, Mark Robson, Teddy Sheringham, Sergei Rebrov and Calum Davenport.

MOST COMMON SURNAME

There have been five Robsons who've played for West Ham, but the most common surname has been Smith. Wing-half John Smith was by far and away the most successful; he clocked up 130 appearances and 22 goals.

David Smith..............A forward who played one game in 1919 against Stoke City
Harry Smith..............Inside-left; played once, against Manchester United in 1927
John Smith........................Wing-half; transferred to Tottenham Hotspur in 1960
Mark Smith......................Just the one game at left-back in 1979, against Swansea
Roy Smith............................Born in India; two appearances in 1956 as a forward
Steve Smith .... Outside-left; made 27 league appearances, 1919 to 1922
Sydney Smith......................................Inside-right; made two appearances in 1904
William Smith ....Full-back who played just twice, in 1929

RECORD-BREAKING SEASON

Season 1980/81 was an amazing campaign for the Hammers, as they romped to the Second Division Championship, winning it by 13 points. In doing so, they achieved seven new club records. The total of 66 points was a post-war record for the Second Division in the two-points-for-a-win era, but the club also set the following records:

Undefeated in 18 successive league games home and away
Won 19 home league games, 16 of which were successive
Won 28 games in the league
Suffered only four league defeats
Kept 22 clean sheets in the League
A goal difference of plus 50

SIX OF THE BEST

The England squad of 2005/06 contained six ex-West Ham players, namely Michael Carrick, Joe Cole, Jermain Defoe, Rio Ferdinand, David James, and Frank Lampard.

BIGGEST WINS

West Ham's record victories are as follows:

10-0 v Bury	League Cup	25 October 1983
8-0 v Rotherham United	Division Two	8 March 1958
8-0 v Sunderland	Division One	19 October 1968
8-2 v Leeds United	Division One	9 February 1929
7-0 v Arsenal	Division One	7 March 1927
7-0 v Liverpool	Division One	1 September 1930
7-0 v Leeds United	League Cup	7 November 1966

STAND-IN GOALKEEPERS

There have been a few instances when outfield players have played in goal, due to injuries or red cards. Playing against Arsenal in April 1962, Lawrie Leslie hurt his hand and was replaced by John Lyall. Leslie later came back to play on the wing – no substitutes were allowed in those days – and he helped West Ham draw 3-3. Three days later at Cardiff City, stand-in keeper Brian Rhodes dislocated his shoulder. This time, Martin Peters went in goal, but Cardiff ran out 3-0 winners. In January 1972, against Stoke City in a League Cup semi-final, goalkeeper Bobby Ferguson went off concussed, and Bobby Moore went in goal. Ferguson returned, but not before Moore had to face a penalty; he saved, but Bernard scored from the rebound and West Ham were beaten 3-2. Against Leeds United in April 1973, Bermudan Clyde Best went in goal after Bobby Ferguson went off concussed. The teams drew 1-1. At Everton in December 1995, goalkeeper Ludek Miklosko was sent off and Julian Dicks played in goal – but West Ham lost 3-0.

WARTIME GUESTS

There were many men who appeared as guests for West Ham during World War II. The following are some of the well known players:

Sam Bartram	(Charlton Athletic)
Willie Corbett	(Celtic)
George Curtis	(Arsenal)
Peter Doherty	(Manchester City)
Ted Drake	(Arsenal)
Eddie Hapgood	(Arsenal)
Harold Hobbis	(Charlton Athletic)
Bernard Joy	(Arsenal)
Les Medley	(Tottenham Hotspur)
Tommy Walker	(Chelsea)

THE HAMMERS IN TEXAS

In April 1967, West Ham met the mighty Real Madrid in an exhibition match played at the Houston Astrodome in Texas. The Spaniards and West Ham shared the honour of being the first teams to play on a full-size pitch completely under cover. The crowd of 33,351 were treated to an exciting match which thrilled the American public. Ruiz put Real ahead after five minutes, but a minute later a header from Geoff Hurst brought the equaliser. On nine minutes, Veloso put the Spaniards ahead again, and they held the lead until half-time. Real opened the second half strongly, and scored a third through Amancio. After 68 minutes John Sissons reduced the arrears, but the game ended with the Hammers being beaten 3-2. During the match, there were many substitutions, and all 15 players in the party were given a game. The players who made the trip were: Standen, Mackleworth, Burnett, Charles, Burkett, Kitchener, Bovington, Heffer, Moore, Redknapp, Bennett, Hurst, Sissons, Brabrook.

ACTION REPLAY II

9 February 1929................... West Ham 8 Leeds United 2.................. First Division

The scourge of Leeds United was Vic Watson, who scored an amazing six goals. The Hammers started well, and Collins laid on the first goal for Watson. It was Ruffell who set up the next, also scored by Watson. Leeds then struck back, with first Wainscoat scoring, then an equaliser from Jennings. Just on the hour, Gibbins put West Ham in front following a pass from Earle, and then Watson came into his own, scoring with a right-foot drive, then pouncing on a loose ball to score another. Tommy Yews broke the spell with number six after a solo run, but Watson completed the scoring with two further goals. The Hammers line up was: Ted Hufton, Tommy Hodgson, Alf Earl, Jim Collins, Matt Smailes, Albert Cadwell, Tommy Yews, Stan Earle, Vic Watson, Viv Gibbins, Jimmy Ruffell.

SEASON 1939/40

Preparations for the season began in an unreal atmosphere, as war loomed once more. The Football League season was only three matches old when everyone's worst fears were realised, and the League programme was immediately abandoned. The three matches played were:

Plymouth Argyle (away)	3-1
Fulham (home)	2-1
Leicester City (home)	0-2

YOUNG STARS

West Ham have won the FA Youth Cup on three occasions, and have been runners-up four times. Joe Kirkup, John Lyall, Jack Burkett, Eddie Bovington, Bobby Moore, John Charles, Harry Redknapp, John Sissons, Alvin Martin, Geoff Pike, Alan Curbishley, Paul Allen, Alan Dickens, Rio Ferdinand, Frank Lampard, Michael Carrick, and Joe Cole all played for the Hammers in finals. All of these went on to enjoy successful careers in the game. The aggregate scores of these two-legged finals have been:

1957	Manchester United	2-8
1959	Blackburn Rovers	1-2
1963	Liverpool	6-5
1975	Ipswich Town	1-5
1981	Tottenham Hotspur	2-1
1996	Liverpool	1-4
1999	Coventry City	9-0

PENALTY SHOOT-OUTS

West Ham have been involved in six of the dreaded penalty shoot-outs, being successful in three of them. Beating Aston Villa in 2000, however, was all in vain, as the game was later declared void, when it came to light that West Ham's substitute Manny Omoyinmi had played in an earlier round for Gillingham. Details of the shoot-outs are:

1997/98	FA Cup Fifth Round	Blackburn Rovers (away)	won 5-4
1997/98	FA Cup Sixth Round	Arsenal (home)	lost 4-3
1999/2000	League Cup Fifth Round	Aston Villa (home)	won 5-4
2002/03	League Cup Third Round	Chesterfield (away)	won 5-4
2004/05	FA Cup Fourth Round	Sheffield United (away)	lost 3-1
2005/06	FA Cup Final	Liverpool (Mill. Stadium)	lost 3-1

GOAL FAMINE

In season 1903/04, West Ham played five successive league games without scoring. Another bad run came in 1999/2000, when they played nine successive away games without a goal.

BLACKBURN TO BLACKBURN

Fred Blackburn was born in Blackburn, and his first club was Blackburn Rovers. He joined West Ham in 1905, and went on to play in 227 games scoring 28 goals.

ALL-TIME TOP GOALSCORER

Between 1920 and 1934, Vic Watson scored an amazing 298 league goals, plus 28 in the FA Cup. His best season was 1929/30, when he scored 42 league goals. These included a hat-trick against Leeds United and a pair of hat-tricks against Aston Villa. He was feared by Leeds – in February 1929, he scored six against them in an 8-2 victory. A year later, he scored all the West Ham goals when Leeds were beaten 4-1 in the FA Cup. Vic also holds the record for scoring in successive league games – he scored in ten in a row during the 1924/25 season. In all, he scored an astonishing 13 hat-tricks during his Hammers career.

GEORGE KAY

Centre-half and captain George Kay had a fine career with West Ham, the pinnacle being the 1923 FA Cup Final. His first club was Bolton Wanderers, for whom he played three league games in 1910/11. During the first World War he served in the Royal Garrison Artillery, before joining West Ham in 1919. He made his debut against Barnsley, during the Hammers' first season as a Football League club. George became captain in 1922, and led the team to promotion, and the 1923 cup final. Kay's was the first Hammers player to play more than 200 league games. By the time he left West Ham in 1926 for Stockport County, he had totalled 259 appearances; he only played two league matches for Stockport before going into management with Luton Town. After two seasons at Luton he left to join Southampton in May 1931. At the Dell, he created their first nursery side, and before long, young players were being drafted into the league side. He resigned as manager in May 1936 to take over as manager at Liverpool. Kay then spent 15 seasons at Anfield, guiding them to the Championship in 1947 and the FA Cup Final in 1950. The following year he retired through ill health, and sadly died in April 1954.

FIRST FOOTBALL LEAGUE GAME

West Ham were admitted to the Football League in 1919, with their first match being played against Lincoln City on 30 August. Before an attendance of 20,000, the teams drew 1-1 at Upton Park. The honour of scoring the first league goal went to Jimmy Moyes, who scored the equaliser in the 65th minute. The Hammers team on that special occasion was: Ted Hufton, Bill Cope, Alf Lee, Harry Lane, Alf Fenwick, Jim McCrae, David Smith, Jim Moyes, Syd Puddefoot, Bob Morris, Harry Bradshaw. Their next game was a crushing 7-0 defeat at Barnsley, but they recovered from this to finish in a respectable seventh position in the league.

THE IRISH IMPORTS

Nine players have signed from clubs in Eire or Northern Ireland:

Noel Cantwell .... Cork Celtic 1952
John Carroll .... Limerick 1948
Laurie Conwell .... Portadown 1935
Fred Kearns .... Shamrock Rovers 1949
George Kay .... Distillery 1919
Danny McGowan .... Shelbourne 1948
Tommy Moroney .... Cork United 1947
Frank O'Farrell .... Cork United 1950
Bill Roberts .... Newry Town 1937

HAT-TRICK AT LAST

In season 1972/73, Bryan 'Pop' Robson had scored just twice in eight league
games before he finally scored a hat-trick on Good Friday against Southampton.
He ended the season as the leading goalscorer in Division One with 28 goals.

SOUTHERN LEAGUE CENTURIONS

Players who made over 100 appearances in the Southern League between 1900
and 1915:

Tommy Allison 156
Herbert Ashton 224
William Askew 104
Fred Blackburn 217
Billy Grassam 169
Len Jarvis 133
George Kitchen 184
Frank Piercy 214
Tom Randall 189
Danny Shea 179
Robert Whiteman 136
Dan Woodards 109

BBC AWARD

The BBC TV "Sportsview" Team Award Trophy 1965 was awarded to West
Ham United in recognition of their performance in the European Cup Winners
Cup Final at Wembley Stadium in May 1965.

PRE-MATCH ENTERTAINMENT

Older supporters will look back with affection as they remember the brass band who used to play before the game and at half-time. The first band was the Metropolitan Police Band; over the years other bands have performed, such as the Gas Light & Coke Co Band, the Police K Division Band and the Leyton Silver Band. In September 1966 the British Legion Band made its first appearance and was resident until the 1977/78 season, when they were replaced by music played over the tannoy.

RECORD DEFEATS

For West Ham fans these are games to forget:

2-8 v Blackburn Rovers .... Division One .... 26 December 1963
0-7 v Barnsley............................ Division Two .... 1 September 1919
0-7 v Everton............................. Division One ....22 October 1927
0-7 v Sheffield Wednesday .... Division One .... 28 November 1959

ABANDONED LEAGUE GAMES

Since World War II, there have been five league games abandoned, four of them due to bad weather and one to floodlight failure:

27 November 1948 .... Grimsby Town (home) 1-2
abandoned after 50 minutes
29 March 1952 ....Brentford (away) 1-1
abandoned after 45 minutes
2 January 1954... Stoke City (home) 4-1
abandoned after 83 minutes due to fog
27 December 1965..Aston Villa (away) 0-0
abandoned after 30 minutes
3 November 1997 .... Crystal Palace (home) 2-2
abandoned after 65 minutes

These days, games would not be started if there were really bad conditions. Going back to the game at Brentford in 1952, the conditions were awful. An avalanche of snow had fallen, and continued to fall. The cold was cutting and raw, and when the Brentford players arrived they were astonished to find that the game was still on. At 3pm the West Ham team tumbled out of their coach, and were soon facing arctic conditions. Every one of the 6,000 supporters was huddled under the stand, with the terraces behind the goals empty. The players continued to soldier through thick snow, and the football became a farce. No wonder the game was abandoned at half-time.

BOYS OF '86

The team that played in season 1985/86 finished third in the First Division, narrowly missing out on winning the league. In 2003, they got together again for the purpose of playing games against local opposition for charity. So far, they have played Heybridge Swifts and Thurrock FC in 2003, Clacton Town in 2004, and Canvey Island in 2005. In 2006, there were games against a Football Careers Centre and Witham Town. Supporters of these clubs have been pleased to be able to see old Hammers heroes such as Phil Parkes, Billy Bonds, Tony Gale, Alvin Martin, Alan Devonshire, Tony Cottee, Frank McAvennie, Neil Orr, and Geoff Pike. As well as the games themselves, they have been involved in numerous other fundraising events.

TWO-TIME HAMMERS

These players could not resist the lure of Upton Park, as they all left and returned. Bryan Robson left the club in 1974 and 1979, and the following seasons West Ham won the FA Cup:

Player	Left	Returned
Tony Cottee	1988	1994
Julian Dicks	1993	1994
Don Hutchison	1996	2001
Steve Jones	1994	1996
Frank McAvennie	1987	1988
Syd Puddefoot	1922	1931
Bryan Robson	1974	1976
Lee Bowyer	2003	2006

ACTION REPLAY III

1 September 1930................West Ham 7 Liverpool 0......................First Division.

A bright start for the Hammers resulted in two early goals, from Watson and Earle. The Reds tried to get back in the game, but their finishing was poor. Midway through the second half, the Hammers banged in three goals in five minutes. Watson scored from a Cadwell pass, then Earle scored his own second before James got the fifth, following good play from Earle and Yews. Unsurprisingly, it was the prolific Vic Watson who completed the scoring with two more goals to add to the Merseysiders' misery. The happy Hammers on that day were: Bob Dixon, Alf Earl, Bill Wade, Jim Collins, Jim Barrett, Albert Cadwell, Tommy Yews, Stan Earle, Vic Watson, Wilf James, Jimmy Ruffell.

SIGNED FROM A NON-LEAGUE TEAM

All these players came from the lowest leagues. Alan Devonshire and Len Goulden both went on to play for England:

Ken Bainbridge .... (Leytonstone) 1946
Ernie Gregory............. (Leytonstone) 1946
Doug Bing........................ (Margate) 1951
Fred Dell .... (Dartford) 1936
Alan Devonshire............... (Southall) 1976
Len Goulden .... (Leyton) 1932
Steve Jones....................... (Billericay) 1992
Bill Lansdowne.... (Woodford Town) 1955
Harry Medhurst .... (Woking) 1938
Roy Stroud .... (Hendon) 1951

BIG JIM

In a career spanning 15 seasons, big Jim Barrett played a total of 467 games for West Ham. He started out as a member of the West Ham Boys team, gaining two England Schoolboy caps in 1921. He came to West Ham United in 1923 and two years later, in March 1925, made his debut, against Tottenham Hotspur. He was ever-present for the following two seasons, and was established in the side at centre-half, though he was versatile enough to come forward to score some goals. Indeed, in his career he totalled 53 league and cup goals for the Hammers. In 1928 he was capped for England against Northern Ireland, but disaster struck after only four minutes when he was injured and had to come off. This remains the shortest recorded England international career. Jim played his last league game in September 1938, but continued to play in regional football throughout the war. In 1946, he was in charge of the 'A' team, and played in the same side as his son, also called Jim. He died, aged 63, in November 1970.

BAD AWAY DAYS

In season 1908/09, there were no away wins at all. Only one away game was won in these seasons:

1902/03.............................. lost 9, drawn 5
1925/26........................... lost 15, drawn 5
1932/33........................... lost 17, drawn 3
1937/38........................... lost 11, drawn 9
1960/61........................... lost 14, drawn 6

CHAIRMEN

The ten men who have looked after the club since 1900:

Lazzeluer Johnson	1900-1903
Edwin Smith	1903-1904
Joseph Grisdale	1904-1909
William White	1909-1935
W.J. Cearns	1935-1950
Reg Pratt	1950-1979
Leonard Cearns	1979-1990
Martin Cearns	1990-1992
Terence Brown	1992-2006
Eggert Magnusson	2006-

NON-LEAGUE IN THE FA CUP

On six occasions since joining the Football League, West Ham have drawn non-league opposition in the cup, and each time they have been successful.

1929	Corinthians (home) Round Four 3-0
1933	Corinthians (away, Crystal Palace) Round Three 2-0
1972	Hereford United (away) Round Four 0-0
	Hereford United (home replay) 3-1
1992	Farnborough Town (away) Round Three 1-1
	Farnborough Town (home replay) 1-0
1994	Kidderminster Harriers (away) Round Five 1-0
1997	Emley (home) Round Three 2-1

HOME GROUNDS

The club have had four grounds since their formation as Thames Ironworks in 1895: Hermit Road, September 1895 to October 1896: The ground was situated in Canning Town in East London. It was surrounded by a moat, and temporary canvas fences were erected to shield the play from non-paying spectators. The dressing rooms were a two-minute walk away, at the nearby Marquis Of Salisbury pub; Browning Road, December 1896 to April 1897: In East Ham and described as 'a wilderness'. Memorial Grounds, June 1897 to April 1904: This ground was built in six months at a cost of £20,000. It had facilities for athletics, cycling, tennis and football. There were two pavilions, which could hold 2,200 people. Boleyn Ground, September 1904 to present day: Initially, it had a small grandstand and some covered terracing. It is now a splendid all-seater stadium with room for some 35,500 supporters.

FA CUP THREE, TWO, WON

When West Ham won the FA Cup in 1964, they did so by scoring three goals in every round:

Third Round ....Charlton Athletic, 3-0
Fourth Round ....Leyton Orient, 3-0
Fifth Round...Swindon Town, 3-1
Quarter-final...Burnley, 3-2
Semi-final ....Manchester United, 3-1
Cup Final ....Preston North End, 3-2

While uncannily in 1975, West Ham scored two goals in every round

Third Round ....Southampton, 2-1
Fourth Round ....Swindon Town, 2-1
Fifth Round....................................Queens Park Rangers, 2-1
Quarter-final... Arsenal, 2-0
Semi-final ....Ipswich Town, 2-1
Cup Final ....Fulham, 2-0

In both finals, West Ham fielded teams comprised entirely of Englishmen. At the end of 2006/07, West Ham had taken part in 310 FA Cup games.

WARTIME CUP WINNERS

West Ham won the Football League War Cup in the first wartime season, 1939/40. They played nine games in the competition, with the first two rounds being played over two legs:

First round first leg...Chelsea (h) 3-2
First round second leg.....................................Chelsea (a) 2-0
Second round ....Leicester City (a) 1-1
Second round second leg........................ Leicester City (h) 3-0
Third round ....Huddersfield Town (a) 3-3
Third round replay.......................Huddersfield Town (h) 3-1
Quarter-final....................................Birmingham City (h) 4-2
Semi-final (at Stamford Bridge) ....Fulham 4-3
Final (at Wembley)................................Blackburn Rovers 1-0

A goal from Sam Small won the cup for the Hammers, and the trophy stands proudly at Upton Park to this day. The team was: Herman Conway, Charlie Bicknell, Charlie Walker, Ted Fenton, Dick Walker, Joe Cockroft, Sam Small, Archie Macaulay, George Foreman, Len Goulden, Stan Foxall.

INFLUX OF OVERSEAS PLAYERS

The first foreign Hammer was Clyde Best, arriving from Bermuda in 1969. He had a tough baptism, as there were few black players in those days. A couple of years later, he was joined by Ade Coker, who came from Nigeria. However, the biggest influx of overseas players into the game did not begin until almost 20 years later. At the end of the 2006/07 season, no fewer than 65 overseas players had worn the claret and blue.

Player	Year Joined	Where Born	Lge Apps
Clyde Best	1969	Bermuda	186
Ade Coker	1971	Nigeria	10
Yilmaz Orhan	1975	Cyprus	8
Francois Van Der Elst	1981	Belgium	62
Ludek Miklosko	1989	Czechoslovakia	315
Ray Atteveld	1991	Holland	1
Alex Bunbury	1992	British Guyana	4
Jeroen Boere	1993	Holland	25
Marc Rieper	1994	Denmark	90
Slaven Bilic	1995	Croatia	48
Marco Boogers	1995	Holland	4
Dani Carvalho	1995	Portugal	9
John Harkes	1995	USA	11
Stan Lazaridis	1995	Australia	68
Ilie Dumitrescu	1995	Romania	10
Paulo Futre	1996	Portugal	9
Steve Mautone	1996	Australia	1
Manny Omoyinmi	1996	Nigeria	9
Hugo Porfirio	1996	Portugal	23
Florin Raducioiu	1996	Romania	11
Samassi Abou	1997	Ivory Coast	22
Paulo Alves	1997	Portugal	4
Eyal Berkovic	1997	Israel	65
Craig Forrest	1997	Canada	30
Bernard Lama	1997	France	12
David Terrier	1997	France	1
Chris Coyne	1998	Australia	1
Kaba Diawara	1998	France	11
Marc Keller	1998	France	44
Javier Margas	1998	Chile	22
Ian Feuer	1999	USA	3
Igor Stimac	1999	Croatia	43
Paulo Wanchope	1999	Costa Rica	35
Sasa Ilic	1999	Australia	1

Christian Bassila	2000	France	3
Titi Camara	2000	Guinea	11
Paolo Di Canio	2000	Italy	118
Hayden Foxe	2000	Australia	11
Sebastien Schemmel	2000	France	63
Ragnvald Soma	2000	Norway	7
Rigobert Song	2000	Cameroon	24
Davor Suker	2000	Croatia	11
Hannu Tihinen	2000	Finland	8
Svetoslav Todorov	2000	Bulgaria	14
Laurent Courtois	2001	France	7
Richard Garcia	2001	Australia	8
Vladimir Labant	2001	Slovakia	13
Tomas Repka	2001	Czech Republic	164
Edouard Cisse	2002	France	25
Marc Vivien Foe	2003	Cameroon	38
Pavel Srnicek	2003	Czech Republic	3
Seb Carole	2003	France	1
Youssef Sofiane	2003	France	1
Sergei Rebrov	2004	Ukraine	26
Mauricio Tarrico	2004	Argentina	1
Lionel Scaloni	2005	Argentina	13
Jeremie Aliadiere	2005	France	7
David Bellion	2005	France	8
Yaniv Katan	2005	Israel	6
Yossi Benayoun	2005	Israel	63
John Pantsil	2006	Ghana	5
Jonathan Spector	2006	USA	25
Javier Mascherano	2006	Argentina	5
Carlos Tevez	2006	Argentina	26
Kepa Blanco	2007	Spain	8

LONDON DERBIES: DELIGHT AND MISERY

Everyone loves a local derby, especially if your team wins.

Team	Best	Worst
Arsenal	7-0 home, Mar 1927	1-6 away, Mar 1976
Charlton Athletic	5-0 home, Dec 2000	0-3 away, Mar 1988
Chelsea	4-0 away, Mar 1986	2-6 away, Apr 1966
Crystal Palace	4-0 home, Oct 1972	0-2 home, Apr 1992
Fulham	7-2 home, Feb 1968	0-5 away, Nov 1936
Millwall	3-0 home, Apr 1989	1-4 away, Mar 2004
Tottenham Hotspur	4-0 home, Feb 1964	1-6 home, Aug 1962

WHATEVER HAPPENED TO THE 1980 FA CUP WINNERS

Phil Parkes: He later became the goalkeeping coach at Ipswich Town, Queens Park Rangers and Wycombe Wanderers. Phil is now involved with 'The Boys of 86' team who play in charity games, and is a matchday host at West Ham. He runs his own building company in Wokingham, where he lives.

Ray Stewart: The popular full-back went into coaching in Scotland after leaving the Hammers. He had roles at St Johnstone, Stirling Albion and Livingston. He became manager at Livingston, and later managed Forfar Athletic. Ray is another of the players who attend the 'Boys of 86' events.

Frank Lampard: He became assistant manager at Southend United, and then took up a similar post at West Ham until 2001. Frank is no longer involved in the game, but naturally takes a keen interest in his son's career at Chelsea.

Billy Bonds: The long-serving midfielder was coach and then manager at West Ham until August 1994. He later coached at Reading and Queens Park Rangers, and managed Millwall. He now works in the media for Capital Gold. Bill occasionally turns out for the Charlton veterans team.

Alvin Martin: Alvin later played for Leyton Orient, and was manager at Southend United until March 1999. He now works in the media for Talksport radio, and is another who is involved with the 'Boys of 86'.

Alan Devonshire: The classy midfielder joined Watford after leaving the Hammers. He then went into management with Maidenhead United and Hampton & Richmond FC.

Paul Allen: He left West Ham for a fine career at both Tottenham Hotspur and Southampton. He also had short spells at Luton Town, Stoke City, Swindon Town, Bristol City and finally Millwall. He now works for the PFA with former team-mate Bobby Barnes.

Stuart Pearson: He became assistant manager at West Bromwich Albion and then Bradford City. He still manages teams in the seven-a-side veterans tournaments, and has links with the PFA.

David Cross: The prolific scorer joined Manchester City in 1982, later playing for Oldham Athletic and West Bromwich Albion. He was youth team boss at Blackburn Rovers before becoming assistant manager at Oldham Athletic for a period, under former Hammer Iain Dowie.

Trevor Brooking: The popular long-serving midfielder worked in the media after leaving the Hammers in 1984. He became a West Ham director, and was the club's caretaker manager for two successful spells. He is now the FA's first director of football management.

Geoff Pike: After leaving West Ham in 1987, he played for Notts County and Leyton Orient, and had a spell with Hendon FC. Geoff has since worked for the PFA, where he helps players with their coaching qualifications.

Manager John Lyall served Ipswich Town for a number of years before he settled into happy retirement in Suffolk. It was a great shock to everyone when he sadly died in April 2006. John made a huge impact on the history of West Ham, and was a kind, considerate man.

YOUNGEST PLAYER

The youngest player to play for the club was Billy Williams, who was 16 years 221 days old when he made his debut against Blackpool on 6 May 1922. Some 80 years later, Chris Cohen was 16 years 283 days old when he played against Sunderland on 13 December 2003. The youngest player to captain the side is Nigel Reo-Coker. He was 20 years 141 days old when skippering against Wolverhampton Wanderers on 2 October 2004. At the age of 22, Bobby Moore became England's youngest ever captain when he was put in charge for the game with Czechoslovakia in May 1963.

SOME FINE CRICKETERS

Goalkeeper Jim Standen was an accomplished cricketer. He won a Championship medal with Worcestershire and topped the first-class county bowling averages, taking 64 wickets. In all, he took 313 wickets for Worcestershire between 1960 and 1970. Syd Puddefoot scored 101 runs for Essex back in 1923. George Eastman kept wicket for Essex, and took 29 catches between 1926 and 1929. Ron Tindall was a Surrey man, and in the 1963 season he scored 1063 runs. In total for the county he scored 5383 runs. Eddie Presland played for Essex between 1962 and 1970 and scored 625 runs. Geoff Hurst played for Essex on two occasions in 1962.

EVER-PRESENTS

The best season for players being ever-present was 1958/59, when five players played in every game. These were John Bond, Ken Brown, Noel Cantwell, Mike Grice and Andy Malcolm. Johnny Dick missed only one game, and Malcolm Musgrove played all but two. This level of stability no doubt helped, as they finished sixth in Division One that season.

UNCHANGED TEAM

In 1980/81, West Ham fielded the same team for ten successive games. From November 11th until December 26th, there were nine league games and one League Cup tie, and the team that started them all was: Phil Parkes, Ray Stewart, Frank Lampard, Billy Bonds, Alvin Martin, Alan Devonshire, Pat Holland, Paul Goddard, David Cross, Trevor Brooking, Geoff Pike.

MILESTONE LEAGUE GOALS

500th	Vic Watson	2nd v Bolton W, 10 Dec 1927
1000th	Vic Watson	4th v Fulham, 30 Mar 1934
1500th	Terry Woodgate	2nd v Leeds United, 24 Apr 1948
2000th	Harry Hooper	1st v Bristol Rovers, 10 Mar 1956
2500th	Martin Peters	4th v Manchester City, 8 Sep 1962
3000th	Trevor Brooking	2nd v Wolverhampton W, 24 Mar 1969
3500th	Bryan Robson	2nd v Brighton & HA 28 Oct 1978
4000th	Frank McAvennie	1st v Manchester United, 25 Aug 1986
4500th	Tony Cottee	2nd v Coventry City, 31 Jan 1996
5000th	David Weir (OG)	1st v Everton, 14 Jan 2006

MILESTONE HOME LEAGUE GOALS

500th	Jimmy Ruffell	3rd v Blackpool, 11 Apr 1931
1000th	Vigo Jenson (og)	1st v Hull City, 19 Aug 1950
1500th	Bobby Moore	3rd v Wolverhampton W, 17 Dec 1960
2000th	Kevin Lock	2nd v Everton, 31 Mar 1973
2500th	Frank McAvennie	1st v Nottingham Forest, 2 Sep 1986
3000th	Jermain Defoe	3rd v Sunderland, 20 Apr 2002

MILESTONE AWAY LEAGUE GOALS

500th	Archie Macaulay	1st v West Bromwich A, 10 Dec1938
1000th	Johnny Byrne	2nd v Arsenal, 14 Nov 1964
1500th	Tony Cottee	1st v Everton, 5 May 1986

THEY SKIPPERED THE SIDE

Captains since 1898: Walter Tranter, Tom Bradshaw, Dave Gardner, Frank Piercy, Tom Randall, Alf Leafe; Bill Cope, George Kay, Billy Moore, Jack Hebden, Stan Earle, Jim Barrett, Charlie Bicknell, Dick Walker, Malcolm Allison, Noel Cantwell, Phil Woosnam, Bobby Moore, Billy Bonds, Alvin Martin, Julian Dicks, Ian Bishop, Steve Potts, Steve Lomas, Joe Cole, Christian Dailly, Teddy Sheringham, Nigel Reo-Coker.

CHAMPIONS I

In only their third season, 1897/98, Thames Ironworks were champions of the London League. They were playing at their new home, the Memorial Grounds, sporting colours of blue and white with red socks. On the final day of the season, the Irons beat bottom side 2nd Grenadier Guards 3-1, but then had to wait for the result of Brentford's game with Barking Woodville. The Thames team were overjoyed to find that Brentford had been surprisingly beaten by Barking, and that Thames Ironworks had therefore won the London League championship. The nucleus of the championship side that season was made up of the following players: George Gresham, James Reid, Simon Chisholm, George Neil, A Edwards, Henry Hird, Walter Tranter, Charlie Dove, David Furnell, Robert Hounsell, W Taylor, Bob Heath.

London League Final Table 1897/98

	W	D	L	F	A	Pts
Thames Ironworks	12	3	1	47	15	27
Brentford	12	2	2	43	17	26
Leyton	8	4	4	41	33	20
3rd Grenadier Guards	7	3	6	34	33	17
Ilford	5	7	4	33	25	17
Stanley	5	4	7	22	22	14
Barking Woodville	2	6	8	16	37	10
Bromley	4	2	10	20	49	10
2nd Grenadier Guards	0	3	13	17	42	3

WE WON THE CUP II

In 1975, West Ham beat Fulham 2-0 with an all-English team. Adding to the attraction of this all-London Cup final was the appearance of Hammers legend Bobby Moore in a Fulham shirt – making what proved to be his last appearance on the Wembley stage. Fulham had looked the better side early on, but it was the Hammers who went ahead on the hour. A Jennings shot was blocked by Mellor, but Alan Taylor was on hand to slip the ball into the net. Five minutes later, a Paddon shot was fumbled by Mellor, and there was Taylor again to lash the ball high into the net. The West Ham team for the club's second FA Cup victory was: Mervyn Day, John McDowell, Frank Lampard, Billy Bonds, Tommy Taylor, Kevin Lock, Billy Jennings, Graham Paddon, Alan Taylor, Trevor Brooking, Pat Holland. Goalscoring hero Alan Taylor was in the headlines around the country, but these days he is in the news in a different way – he owns a newsagent's in Norwich.

CHRISTMAS DAY

Up until 1958, clubs used to play on Christmas Day, and then play the same opponents on Boxing Day. A plea from the players to spend this day with their families resulted in Christmas Day fixtures being abandoned. The last time West Ham played on Christmas Day was in 1958, when the Hammers beat their London rivals Tottenham Hotspur 2-1, with goals from Johnny Dick and Vic Keeble. The team line-up was: Gregory, Bond, Cantwell, Malcolm, Brown, Smith, Grice, Smillie, Keeble, Dick, Musgrove.

JAPANESE TOUR 1984

In May and June 1984, the club undertook a tour of Japan, playing five games in a club and national cup which was eventually won by Santos:

Opponents	Venue	Score
Santos (Brazil)	Shimizu	1-2
Japan	Okayama	2-2
Malaysia	Tokyo	9-2
Yomiuri (Japan)	Sapporo	0-0
Uruguay	Nagoya	1-1

100th LEAGUE MEETINGS

Opponents	Venue	Date	Score
Arsenal	away	7 April 2007	1-0
Everton	away	15 March 2003	0-0
Leicester City	home	11 April 1993	3-0
Liverpool	home	30 January 2007	1-2
Manchester United	away	14 December 2002	0-3
Newcastle United	home	12 April 2000	2-1
Nottingham Forest	away	28 December 2003	2-0
Tottenham Hotspur	away	6 December 1999	0-0

HAMMERS IN THE PLAY-OFFS

West Ham have been involved in two end-of-season play-offs campaigns:

2003/04 semi-final	Ipswich Town (a)	0-1
2003/04 semi-final	Ipswich Town (h)	2-0
2003/04 final	Crystal Palace (Millennium Stadium)	0-1
2004/05 semi-final	Ipswich Town (h)	2-2
2004/05 semi-final	Ipswich Town (a)	2-0
2004/05 final	Preston North End (Millennium Stadium)	1-0

HARRY POTTER

West Ham get a mention in one of the famous Harry Potter novels. In chapter nine of *Harry Potter And The Philosopher's Stone* the character Ron Weasley is caught prodding a poster of the West Ham team trying to make the players move. Author J K Rowling explains on her official web site that the reference to the team was because one of her friends is a passionate West Ham United supporter.

HAMMERS IN PRINT

Over the years there has been a fascinating array of Hammers books to include all tastes: autobiographies, complete records, quiz books and illustrated histories.

Title	Author	Year
Let's Talk About West Ham	T Morgan	1946
West Ham History	R Groves	1947
At Home With The Hammers	T Fenton	1960
Strategy Of Soccer	J Byrne	1966
My Soccer Story	B Moore	1966
The World Game	G Hurst	1967
West Ham Football Book I	D Irvine	1968
Goals From Nowhere	M Peters	1969
West Ham Football Book 2	D Irvine	1969
England England	B Moore	1970
Moore On Mexico	B Moore	1970
West Ham Football Book 3	D Irvine	1970
Colours Of My Life	M Allison	1975
Bobby Moore	J Powell	1976
Balls	J Byrne	1976
Champions	H Harris	1981
Trevor Brooking Autobiography	T Brooking	1981
Official Annual	H Harris	1981
Official Annual	H Harris	1982
Official Annual	C Benson	1983
Yours Sincerely	R Greenwood	1984
West Ham Story	J Moynihan	1984
Official Annual	C Benson	1984
West Ham United	C Korr	1986
Who's Who	T Hogg & J Helliar	1986
A Complete Record	J Northcutt & R Shoesmith	1987
Bonzo	B Bonds	1988
West Ham Quiz Book	T Hogg	1988
Just Like My Dreams	J Lyall	1989
Hammers Annual	T McDonald	1990

West Ham Quiz Book	D Standing	1991
Soccer Quiz Series West Ham	J Northcutt	1991
Bobby Moore Life And Times	J Powell	1993
Bobby Moore	D Emery	1993
Illustrated History	J Northcutt & R Shoesmith	1994
Claret And Blues	T Cottee	1995
100 Years Of Football	T Hogg & T McDonald	1995
An Irrational Hatred Of Luton	R Banks	1995
Who's Who	T Hogg & T McDonald	1995
Julian Dicks Terminator	K Blows	1996
Moore Than A Legend	P Daniels	1997
Youth Soccer Coaching	T Carr	1997
Bubbles Hammers And Dreams	B Belton	1997
Gatling Gun George Hilsdon	C Kerrigan	1997
Hammers Dream Team	J Tomas	1997
West Ham Match By Match	C Leatherdale	1998
West Ham Yearbook	S Bradley and others	1998
Upton Park Encyclopedia	D Hayes	1998
West Ham 25 Year Record	D Powter	1998
Hammers In Focus	S Bacon	1998
Harry Redknapp Autobiography	H Redknapp	1998
First And Last Englishmen	B Belton	1998
Official History	A Ward	1999
Fortunes Always Hiding	K Blows	1999
Hell Razor	N Ruddock	1999
Days Of Iron	B Belton	1999
The Hard Way	R Slater	1999
West Ham Till I Die	R Banks	2000
P DiCanio Autobiography	P DiCanio	2000
Essential History	K Blows & T Hogg	2000
Psycho	S Pearce	2000
The Elite Era	J Helliar	2000
1966 And All That	G Hurst	2001
Boys Of 86	T McDonald & D Francis	2001
You Have Just Met The ICF	C Pennant	2002
Rio	W Clarkson	2002
Irons In The Soul	P May	2002
Want Some Aggro	C Pennant & N Smith	2002
Claret And Blue Blood	K Blows & B Sharratt	2002
Scoring An Experts Guide	F McAvennie	2003
The Definitive West Ham	J Northcutt	2003
The Legacy Of Barry Green	R Banks	2003
West Ham Utd Collection	No Author named	2003
Founded On Iron	B Belton	2003

West Ham Dream Team	A Ward & D Smith	2003
Johnnie The One	B Belton	2004
For The Claret And Blue	N Smith	2004
Burn Budgie Byrne	B Belton	2004
Nightmare On Green Street	P Thorne	2004
Our Days Are Few	M Godleman	2004
Hammers Annual	J Helliar and Others	2004
Iron in the Blood	J Powles	2005
Good Afternoon Gentlemen	B Gardner	2005
Frank Lampard	D Thompson	2005
Bobby Moore	T Moore	2005
Nearly Reached The Sky	S Blowers	2005
The Men Of 64	B Belton	2005
Hammers Annual	D Clayton	2005
Hammers in the Heart	P May	2005
Whos Who	T Hogg	2005
Holmes Coaching Manual	Matty Holmes	2005
West Ham Quiz Book	C Cowlin	2006
How to coach a soccer team	T Carr	2006
World Champions	G Hurst	2006
The Ghost of 66	M Peters	2006
The Black Hammers	B Belton	2006
Totally Frank	F Lampard	2006
West Ham Miscellany	B Belton	2006
Rio My Story	R Ferdinand	2006
Cole Play	I Macleay	2006
West Ham Annual	C Benson	2006
Through The Looking Glass	M Godleman	2006
Lads Of 23	B Belton	2006
Rio My Story	R Ferdinand	2006
Cole Play	I Macleay	2006
West Ham Annual	C Benson	2006
Through The Looking Glass	M Godleman	2006
Lads Of 23	B Belton	2006
The Little Book Of West Ham Utd.	D Russell	2006

BEST-EVER START

West Ham started the 1990/91 season unbeaten for 21 league games. The run started on 25 August with a 0-0 draw at Middlesborough, and came to an end with a 1-0 defeat at Barnsley on 22 December. There were eight draws and 13 wins. The team won promotion at the end of that season.

BOMB DAMAGE

In August 1944, a flying bomb caused extensive damage to the roof of the South Bank. The first 14 league games were therefore played on opponents' grounds. The first game back at the Boleyn took place on 2 December 1944 against Tottenham Hotspur.

CHAMPIONS II

Season 1957/58 saw West Ham win the Second Division Championship. From the time Vic Keeble came from Newcastle United in October, the goals flowed. He forged a good partnership with Johnny Dick, and between them they scored 40 league goals. The Hammers managed six-goal hauls against Bristol Rovers, Lincoln City and Swansea Town, while Rotherham United were hammered 8-0. The title was clinched on the final day of the season, when the Hammers won 3-1 at Middlesborough. They scored a total of 101 league goals in an exciting campaign which finished with the club's first championship as a league club.

Football League Second Division 1957/58

	W	D	L	F	A	Pts
West Ham United	23	11	8	101	54	57
Blackburn Rovers	22	12	8	93	57	56
Charlton Athletic	24	7	11	107	69	55
Liverpool	22	10	10	79	54	54
Fulham	20	12	10	97	59	52
Sheffield United	21	10	11	75	50	52
Middlesbrough	19	7	16	83	74	45
Ipswich Town	16	12	14	68	69	44
Huddersfield Town	14	16	12	63	66	44
Bristol Rovers	17	8	17	85	80	42
Stoke City	18	6	18	75	73	42
Leyton Orient	18	5	19	77	79	41
Grimsby Town	17	6	19	86	83	40
Barnsley	14	12	16	70	74	40
Cardiff City	14	9	19	63	77	37
Derby County	14	8	20	60	81	36
Bristol City	13	9	20	63	88	35
Rotherham United	14	5	23	65	101	33
Swansea Town	11	9	22	72	99	31
Lincoln City	11	9	22	55	82	31
Notts County	12	6	24	44	80	30
Doncaster Rovers	8	11	23	56	88	27

DOUBLE BOOKED

In November 1901 West Ham found themselves having to play two games on the same day. The fixture list showed that Tottenham Hotspur were the visitors in a Southern League game, but a blunder was made, and an official arranged for Leyton to visit in a FA Cup tie. The prospect of a good attendance for the visit of Spurs could not be ignored, and the Hammers solved the problem by waiving home advantage in the Cup, sending their reserve team to Leyton... where they won 1-0. The first team lost 1-0, but attracted a huge gate of 17,000, which must have pleased the chairman.

THE HAMMERS ARE BORN

Back in 1900, Thames Ironworks needed to go public in an effort to raise capital. Four thousand ten shilling (50p) shares were offered to staff, and later to the general public. In June, Thames Ironworks FC resigned from the Southern League and were wound up. On 5 July 1900, the club was reformed under the new name of West Ham United. Subscribers to the Articles of Incorporation were:

> Aitken Brown .... (Brass Founder)
> J. Cearns .... (Clerk)
> George Fundell .... (House Agent)
> George Handley .... (Contractor)
> Lazzeluer Johnson .... (Clerk)
> Cornelius Osborn .... (Clerk)
> Edwin Smith .... (Timber Convertor)

They were joined by three others to form the first board of directors:

> John Byford .... (Merchant)
> Albert Davis .... (Engineer)
> George Hone .... (Patentee)

THINGS THEY SAID II

In 2000, Paolo Di Canio wrote in his biography:

'We have an outstanding crop of players at West Ham. Michael Carrick is one of my favourite players. He is the kind of player you build championship sides around. Joe Cole is one of the greatest talents of the past 20 years. He has the opportunity to become one of the top players in the world. The best centre-half in the world is Lazio's Nesta but I believe that Rio Ferdinand can become as good or even better than him.'

RECORD VICTORY

West Ham beat Bury 10-0 in a League Cup second round match on 25 October 1983, played at Upton Park. The Hammers were leading 2-1 from the first leg, but few in the crowd of 10,896 expected a massacre. Teenager Tony Cottee scored four, with midfield stars Trevor Brooking and Alan Devonshire bagging two apiece. Alvin Martin scored from a header, and Ray Stewart got on the scoresheet from the penalty spot. Luckless Bury missed a penalty when Bramhall's shot rebounded off a post. It was West Ham's biggest victory, but ironically it was watched by their smallest-ever crowd for a home cup tie. The Hammers team was: Phil Parkes, Ray Stewart, Steve Walford, Billy Bonds, Alvin Martin, Alan Devonshire, Paul Allen, Tony Cottee, Dave Swindlehurst, Trevor Brooking, Geoff Pike.

AMERICAN SOCCER LEAGUE

In 1963, West Ham were invited, along with 13 other overseas teams, to participate in a tournament in America. The teams were split into two leagues, with the winners of each league playing each other over two legs. West Ham only lost one of their six league matches, and finished top of their group. The details of those games were:

Opponents	Score	Scorer(s)
Kilmarnock (Scotland)	3-3	Brabrook, Hurst, Peters.
Mantova (Italy)	2-4	Hurst, Sealey.
Oro (Mexico)	3-1	Hurst 2, Byrne
Valenciennes (France)	3-1	Hurst 3
Preussen Munster (West Germany)	2-0	Peters, Hurst.
Recife (Brazil)	1-1	Byrne

In the group play-offs West Ham beat the Polish team Gornik 2-1 on aggregate. The first match finished 1-1, with a goal from Johnny Byrne. In the second game, the Hammers won 1-0 with Geoff Hurst being the scorer – his ninth of the tournament.

AMERICAN CHALLENGE CUP

After beating Gornik, West Ham qualified to meet Dukla Prague from Czechoslovakia over two legs in the American Challenge Cup. The first leg was played before 11,000 spectators at Soldier Field in Chicago. A first-half goal gave Dukla a narrow 1-0 victory. There was a 15,000 crowd at Randalls Island Stadium in New York for the return. Tony Scott put West Ham ahead, but the Czechs scored a late equaliser to win the cup.

CHAMPIONS III

West Ham raced away with the Second Division Championship in 1980/81, winning it by a clear 13 points. Preston North End and Bristol City were both beaten 5-0, while Grimsby Town suffered a 5-1 home defeat. Top league goalscorers were David Cross, with 22 goals, and Paul Goddard who claimed 17 goals. It was a great season, as the team also reached the League Cup Final, narrowly losing 2-1 to Liverpool in a replay.

Football League Second Division 1980/81

	W	D	L	F	A	Pts
West Ham United	28	10	4	79	29	66
Notts County	18	17	7	49	38	53
Swansea City	18	14	10	64	44	50
Blackburn Rovers	16	18	8	42	29	50
Luton Town	18	12	12	61	46	48
Derby County	15	15	12	57	52	45
Grimsby Town	15	15	12	44	42	45
Queens Park Rangers	15	13	14	56	46	43
Watford	16	11	15	50	45	43
Sheffield Wednesday	17	8	17	53	51	42
Newcastle United	14	14	14	30	45	42
Chelsea	14	12	16	46	41	40
Cambridge United	17	6	19	53	66	40
Shrewsbury Town	11	17	14	46	47	39
Oldham Athletic	12	15	15	39	48	39
Wrexham	12	14	16	43	45	38
Orient	13	12	17	52	56	38
Bolton Wanderers	14	10	18	61	66	38
Cardiff City	12	12	18	44	60	36
Preston North End	11	14	17	41	62	36
Bristol City	7	16	19	29	51	30
Bristol Rovers	5	13	24	34	65	23

BOBBY THE WHISTLE BLOWER

A strange incident occurred during the home game on 14 November 1970 against Wolverhampton Wanderers. With ten minutes remaining, a clearance from Bobby Moore flew straight into the face of referee John Lewis. The force was enough to knock the official out cold. Seeing the referee unconscious, Bobby took the whistle from his hand and blew it to halt the game. The dazed official needed several minutes' treatment before he was able to restart the game.

THE WHITE HORSE FINAL

The 1923 FA Cup Final became known as the White Horse Final. It was being held at the new Wembley Stadium for the first time. Thousands of enthusiastic fans made their way to the stadium, unaware of the drama that was to follow. The ground was soon full to capacity, and the gates were locked. This did not put a stop to the chaos, as thousands just climbed over the walls, or broke down barriers in their desire to get inside. Many fans then left the terraces for refuge on the pitch, and it seemed that the game would never go ahead. Then onto the pitch came a police inspector, riding the famous white horse called Billie. Gradually, he was able to get the fans back to the touchlines, and the game eventually started at 3.44pm. Bolton started strongly, and took the lead after just three minutes with a goal from David Jack. West Ham's strength lay with their wingers Richards and Ruffell, but with the fans standing on the touchline it was very difficult to play on the wings. Eight minutes into the second half, Smith scored Bolton's second goal, and they went on to win the cup. It was estimated that there were around 200,000 spectators inside the ground, although the official attendance was given as 126,047. The West Ham team travelled back to Canning Town in an illuminated tramcar decorated in claret and blue, and despite the defeat they were met by thousands of happy supporters. West Ham lined up as follows: Ted Hufton, Billy Henderson, Jack Young, Syd Bishop, George Kay, Jack Tresadern, Dick Richards, Billy Brown, Vic Watson, Billy Moore, Jimmy Ruffell.

TEST MATCHES

In their first Southern League season, 1898/99, Thames Ironworks were involved in a Test match against Sheppey United. Thames had won Division Two, and Sheppey had finished second from bottom in Division One. A goal from David Lloyd gave Thames a 1-1 draw. A replay was not needed, as it was decided to enlarge the senior league to accommodate them both. The following season, after finishing second from bottom, Thames were again involved with a Test Match. This time it was against Fulham, who were runners up in the Second Division. A hat-trick from Bill Joyce, and further goals from Stewart and Head, gave the Irons a 5-1 win.

CHAMPIONS SCULPTURE

On 28 April 2003, Prince Andrew, HRH The Duke of York, unveiled the 'Champions' sculpture, which depicts the England 1966 World Cup victory. The sculpture is of England stars Geoff Hurst, Martin Peters and Ray Wilson holding aloft Bobby Moore. It dominates the junction of Green Street and the Barking Road, some 100 yards from the club gates.

PENALTY-KICK EXPERT

Scottish full-back Ray Stewart was the best penalty kick taker in West Ham's history. He scored an amazing 76 penalties, missing only ten. From two of those ten, he scored from the rebound after saves by the goalkeeper. Spread over ten seasons, he scored penalties in 57 league fixtures, 12 League Cup ties, six FA Cup matches, and one European Cup Winners Cup game. Two crucial penalties were scored in the last minute. One was in the FA Cup quarter-final in 1980, when he scored against Aston Villa to give the Hammers a 1-0 victory. The other one came at Wembley in the League Cup Final against Liverpool in 1981. He coolly scored with the last kick of the match to give West Ham an equalising goal. Ray was a great player who made 431 appearances for the club. His ferocious shooting also netted him eight other goals from free-kicks and open play.

TED HUFTON

Ted Hufton was born at Southwell, Nottinghamshire on 25 November 1892. One of the best goalkeepers to play for the club, he once saved 11 out of 18 spot kicks over two seasons. His early career was spent at Sheffield United, where he made 16 appearances in 1912. When war broke out, Ted joined the Coldstream Guards, and was wounded in action in France. While recuperating, he guested for West Ham on 53 occasions, and this led to his eventual transfer to the Hammers for £350 in 1919. He was in the side for West Ham's first-ever game in the Football League against Lincoln City in August 1919. Ted was also in goal when the Hammers reached Wembley in 1923 for the first FA Cup Final there. His excellent displays soon gained recognition from the England selectors, and over the next few seasons he was capped six times. He went on to play in 402 games for West Ham before being transferred to Watford in 1932. Ted broke a finger in a pre-season practice game, and only played two games for the Hornets. He later returned to Upton Park as a press-room steward for a number of years, and died in Swansea in February 1967.

SOUTHERN FLOODLIGHT CUP

West Ham played in this competition from 1955 until 1960. In those days, it was considered a first-team competition. West Ham won the inaugural competition, when they beat Aldershot 2-1 in the final at Upton Park in April 1955. Geoff Hurst made his senior debut against Fulham in the competition in December 1958; in 1959, Harry Obeney scored four goals in a 6-1 victory against Reading. In 1960, during the last season of the competition, the Hammers reached the final, but lost 2-1 to Coventry City at Highfield Road, in a match watched by 16,921 spectators.

FLOODLIT FRIENDLIES

In the 1950s and 1960s, West Ham, as was common with clubs not in European competitions, played a series of home floodlit friendlies.

Date	Opponents	Outcome
April 1953	St Mirren	3-3
October 1953	Sunderland	2-0
October 1953	Heart of Midlothian	7-0
February 1954	St Mirren	3-1
April 1954	Servette (Switzerland)	5-1
April 1954	Olaria (Brazil)	0-0
October 1954	Stuttgart (West Germany)	4-0
October 1954	SC Wacker (Austria)	3-1
December 1954	AC Milan (Italy)	0-6
January 1955	Portsmouth	4-1
February 1955	SC Simmering (Austria)	8-2
March 1955	Holland Sports Club (Holland)	0-0
October 1955	Distillery (N Ireland)	7-5
November 1955	SK Rapid (Austria)	1-1
April 1956	Kaiserslautern (West Germany)	2-4
March 1957	Sparta Prague (Czechoslovakia)	3-3
October 1957	Sparta Rotterdam (Holland)	5-0
November 1957	LKS Lodz (Poland)	4-1
October 1959	FC Austria (Austria)	2-0
November 1959	UDA Dukla (Czechoslovakia)	1-1
April 1960	Fluminense (Brazil)	5-4

FOUR PENS IN THREE DAYS

Geoff Hurst once scored four penalties in three days. On 12 March 1969, he scored two for England against France at Wembley. He repeated the feat on 14 March, playing for West Ham against Coventry City

WORLD WAR ONE JOTTINGS

In 1916/17, playing at right-back for three games was a player named as Day. He was a guest player and did not want his real name revealed. It was, however, rumoured that he was Jesse Pennington, an international full-back who was with West Bromwich Albion. In the 1917/18 season West Ham used six goalkeepers. That year, the news came through from France that Arthur Stallard and Bill Kennedy had been killed in action. Both of them had played for West Ham in the Southern League. In 1918/19, West Ham called upon 62 players, a club record.

LONG SERVICE

A number of players gave long service to the club in other capacities after retiring from playing. In 1922, Billy Moore joined West Ham from Sunderland. He played in a total of 202 games, scoring 48 goals, and became the club's trainer in 1929, a job he held until 1960 - a total period of 38 years with the club. Wally St Pier came to the club in 1929, and had made 24 league appearances before being made chief scout four years later, a position he held until 1976. Former goalkeeper Ernie Gregory first joined the ground staff in 1936, and as a player he represented the club in 406 league and cup games. He then became the club's coach, and later looked after the goalkeepers. When he officially retired in 1987, he had spent an incredible 51 years at Upton Park. Eddie Chapman signed for West Ham in 1937, and as a player made seven league appearances, scoring three goals. He became the club's secretary in 1956, and later was appointed chief executive. When he left West Ham in 1986, he had been with them for 49 years. John Lyall joined the ground staff in 1956, but an injury cut short his playing career in 1963 after 35 appearances. He joined the club's coaching staff, and became manager in 1974. He was in charge when the Hammers won the FA Cup in 1975 and 1980. In 1989, following the club's relegation, John was dismissed after 33 years' loyal service. He later managed Ipswich Town for a few seasons.

BOBBY MOORE MEMORIAL MATCH

This game took place at Upton Park on 7 March 1994, and heralded the official opening of the Bobby Moore Stand. West Ham played a FA Premier League XI on a magical night of nostalgia and respect for a great man. Before the game, Stephanie Moore, his widow, unveiled a bronze bust of Bobby, which still takes pride of place at the ground today. The opening ceremony was carried out by the 1964 FA Cup-winning side. They cut claret and blue ribbons in front of the stand, and released 2,000 ballons. There was a moving one-minute silence before kick-off at 8pm. In the game itself Tony Cottee, at that time an Everton player, put the visiting selection ahead. Clive Allen equalised, and Jeroen Boere scored the winner nine minutes from the end. Both teams were presented with medals after the match, and the 20,311 fans returned home happy. The Hammers team on the night included many substitutions, and the following players all took part in a memorable occasion: Ludek Miklosko, Peter Butler, Dale Gordon, Steve Potts, Alvin Martin, Ian Bishop, Martin Allen, Trevor Morley, Matt Holmes, Tony Gale, Clive Allen, Keith Rowland, Kenny Brown, Steve Jones, Danny Williamson, Jeroen Boere, Gary Kelly.

SOUTHERN LEAGUE CHARACTERS

Harry Stapley played for the Hammers from 1905 until 1908, scoring 39 goals in 71 league appearances. He topped the goalscoring lists for three successive seasons. Harry then joined Second Division Glossop, and was top goalscorer there for a further seven successive seasons – an incredible feat, largely overlooked in record books. A brilliant inside forward, Danny Shea scored 111 goals in 179 Southern League appearances for West Ham. In 1913 Blackburn Rovers broke the existing transfer record to take him to Ewood Park for £2,000. While with the Rovers, he won a First Division championship medal and two England caps, returning to West Ham in 1920. George Webb was the first West Ham player to win an England international cap when he played against Scotland and Wales in 1911. He was an amateur, and only played for the club when his business as a toy manufacturer allowed. With the Hammers, he made 52 appearances, scoring 23 goals. George sadly died at the young age of 28 in March 1915.

CHARLIE PAYNTER

This grand gentleman spent a total of 50 years with West Ham as trainer and manager. He came to the club in 1900 as assistant trainer. When Tom Robinson retired in 1912, Charlie took over as trainer, with former captain Frank Piercy as his assistant. Charlie kept the job for 20 years. He was an ideal link between the players and the manager, and was respected throughout football. Charlie was selected to take charge of the England team for their game against Scotland at Wembley in 1924. He was appointed Hammers manager in 1932, following the death of Syd King. He got together a promising side, but war intervened to halt their progress. In 1940, he led the side that won the Football League War Cup, and retired in 1950 after recommending that Ted Fenton be made manager. The board granted him a testimonial in September 1950. A turnout of 18,000 watched West Ham beat Arsenal 3-1.

WE WON THE CUP III

Second Division West Ham faced their London rivals Arsenal at Wembley in 1980. After 13 minutes, Trevor Brooking stooped low to head West Ham into the lead. Arsenal came back into the game, with the Hammers having to rely mainly on counter-attacks. The West Ham defence stood firm, with Bonds and Martin outstanding. Arsenal were frustrated, and the cup came back to the East End. The Hammers team on that great day was: Phil Parkes, Ray Stewart, Frank Lampard, Billy Bonds, Alvin Martin, Alan Devonshire, Paul Allen, Stuart Pearson, David Cross, Trevor Brooking, Geoff Pike.

FANZINES

In the late 1980s, fans around the country started issuing their own club magazines, which became known as fanzines. Like most clubs, West Ham have over the years had many fanzines devoted to them, some of which only lasted for a few issues. Here is a list of a few of them: The Cockney Pride, The East End Connection, The Loyal Supporter, UTD United, The Boleyn Scorcher, Never Mind The Boleyn, Forever Blowing Bubbles, Ultimate Truth, We Ate All The Pies, Fortunes Always Hiding, The Ultimate Dream, On A Mission From God, The Water In Majorca, On The Terraces. None of them exists today, but there are two which deserve a special mention. Over Land and Sea reached issue number 417 in May 2007 and gives fans' opinions and player interviews, and covers all first-team matters. The Ironworks Gazette reached edition number 171 in May 2007. This is more of a club magazine than a fanzine. It covers all first-team matters, and also concentrates on the reserves, youth team and even the ladies' teams.

ESSEX PROFESSIONAL CUP

West Ham played in this competition for nine seasons, and always fielded their first team. They reached the final on five occasions:

Year	Opponents	Outcome
1951	Southend United (h)	2-0
1952	Colchester United (a)	1-3
1954	Southend United (a)	3-3*
1958	Chelmsford City (a)	1-5
1959	Leyton Orient (h)	4-1

* the clubs shared the trophy

GIANTKILLERS

Back in season 1910/11, West Ham were playing in the Southern League. In the FA Cup, they reached the third round, where the draw paired them with the mighty Manchester United. The United team were top of the First Division at the time, and their team was packed with internationals. The Hammers went ahead after nine minutes, when Danny Shea drove the ball home, but the illustrious visitors equalised just before half-time with a goal from Turnbull. West Ham played well in the second half, but as the game was nearing the end it seemed that a replay would be needed. However, in the dying seconds Tommy Caldwell was on hand to smack the winner past Edmonds. The 27,000 crowd were ecstatic, and carried Caldwell shoulder-high from the pitch.

WHAT A SPECTACLE

Stanley Bourne played in 13 league games between 1906 and 1911 and was the only footballer, other than goalkeepers, known to have worn spectacles during a professional match.

CHAMPIONS OF EUROPE

West Ham qualified for the European Cup Winners Cup in 1965 and on a glorious evening in May lifted the trophy:

Stage	Opponents	Outcome
First round	La Gantoise (Belgium) (a)	1-1
First round	La Gantoise (Belgium) (h)	1-0
Second round	Sparta Prague (Czechoslovakia) (h)	2-0
Second round	Sparta Prague (Czechoslovakia) (a)	1-2
Quarter-final	Lausanne (Switzerland) (a)	2-1
Quarter-final	Lausanne (Switzerland) (h)	4-3
Semi-final	Real Zaragoza (Spain) (h)	2-1
Semi-final	Real Zaragoza (Spain) (a)	1-1
Final	TSV Munich (West Germany)	2-0

The final was played at Wembley, where two goals from Alan Sealey gave West Ham victory. The team on that memorable night was: Jim Standen, Joe Kirkup, Jack Burkett, Martin Peters, Ken Brown, Bobby Moore, Alan Sealey, Ronnie Boyce, Geoff Hurst, Brian Dear, John Sissons.

CLUB MUSEUM

The museum opened on 24 August 2002, and contains an amazing array of photographs and memorabilia relating to the club's golden heritage. The focal point of the museum is the incredible 'Champions' collection of medals, caps, jerseys, and trophies won by three of West Ham's greatest legends, Bobby Moore, Geoff Hurst and Martin Peters. Included in the collection are their three World Cup medals. The shirt worn by full-back Jack Young in the 1923 FA Cup Final is also on show, while around the ground you can see the Johnny Byrne collection, comprising his England caps and FA Cup and League Cup medals.

THORN IN OUR SIDE

Between 1961 and 1966, the Blackburn striker John Byrom scored 12 goals against West Ham. This included three hat-tricks. Perhaps fortunately, he was not playing when the Hammers lost 8-2 to Rovers in 1963.

GOING UP I

Season 1922/23 ended in promotion to the First Division for the first time. This was also the year that the Hammers reached the FA Cup Final. There was an exciting end to the campaign, as on the last day West Ham, Leicester City and Notts County were all level on 51 points, and County were also the visitors to Upton Park. Leicester kicked off early, and news of their defeat was relayed to the ground, setting off wild scenes, as that meant that regardless of the result both teams were promoted. Unfortunately for the Hammers, they lost 1-0 and finished runners-up. Top goalscorers were Vic Watson, with 22 goals, and Billy Moore who scored 15.

Football League Second Division 1922/33

	W	D	L	F	A	Pts
Notts County	23	7	12	46	34	53
West Ham United	20	11	11	63	38	51
Leicester City	21	9	12	65	44	51
Manchester United	17	14	11	51	36	48
Blackpool	18	11	13	60	43	47
Bury	18	11	13	55	46	47
Leeds United	18	11	13	43	36	47
Sheffield Wednesday	17	12	13	54	47	46
Barnsley	17	11	14	62	51	45
Fulham	16	12	14	43	32	44
Southampton	14	14	14	40	40	42
Hull City	14	14	14	43	45	42
South Shields	15	10	17	35	44	40
Derby County	14	11	17	46	50	39
Bradford City	12	13	17	41	45	37
Crystal Palace	13	11	18	54	62	37
Port Vale	14	9	19	39	51	37
Coventry City	15	7	20	46	63	37
Clapton Orient	12	12	18	40	50	36
Stockport County	14	8	20	43	58	36
Rotherham County	13	9	20	44	63	35
Wolverhampton W	9	9	24	42	77	27

GUINNESS WORLD RECORD

The West Ham fans were officially entered into the Guinness Book Of World Records. They set a world record for the largest number of people to blow bubbles simultaneously for one minute: 23,680 at Upton Park before the game against Middlesbrough on 16 May 1999.

INTERTOTO GLORY

For West Ham to play in the UEFA Cup in 1999, they had to win a place via the Intertoto Cup. This they did, on that marvellous evening in Metz in August 1999. Results along the way were:

Opponents	First leg	Second leg
Jokerit (Finland)	home 1-0	away 1-1
Heerenveen (Holland)	home 1-0	away 1-0
Metz (France)	home 0-1	away 3-1

Sinclair, Wanchope and Lampard were the scorers in Metz, and the Hammers team on that night was: Shaka Hislop, Steve Lomas, Marc Keller, Marc Vivien Foe, Rio Ferdinand, Steve Potts, Trevor Sinclair, John Moncur, Paulo Wanchope. Paolo DiCanio, Frank Lampard. Joe Cole came on as substitute.

ACTION REPLAY IV

12 February 2000 .... West Ham 5 Bradford City 4 .... Premier League

The drama began after two minutes, when goalkeeper Shaka Hislop broke his leg. On came 18-year-old Stephen Bywater to make his debut. After half an hour, Bradford took the lead when Dean Windass headed in from six yards, but just five minutes later West Ham were back in the game, Trevor Sinclair smashing home the equaliser. Moments before the interval, John Moncur fired home a stunning goal to give the Hammers the lead. However, just seconds later Moncur turned from hero to villain by barging Dean Saunders inside the area, and a penalty was awarded. Peter Beagrie tucked it away, and honours were even at half time. Two minutes after the restart, Bywater failed to hold a shot, and Jamie Lawrence put the Bantams ahead once more. Within three minutes, Lawrence scored again, and Bradford were in control. Paul Kitson was then brought down, and from the resultant penalty Paolo DiCanio pulled a goal back. Four minutes later, the crowd went wild as Joe Cole scored his first league goal to level the scores, and with seven minutes remaining Frank Lampard curled a shot into the top corner to complete an amazing comeback.

1000th LEAGUE WIN

On 3 December 1988, Paul Ince scored in a 1-0 victory against Millwall at the Den. It was a milestone achievement, being the Hammers' 1,000th win in the Football League since they made their competition debut in a Second Division home game against Lincoln City in August 1919.

BITS AND PIECES FROM THE EIGHTIES

In the match programme for the League Cup tie with Bury in October 1983, Bury manager Jim Iley is quoted as saying: "We will surprise a lot of people tonight and will give it everything. There is no question of us coming to Upton Park to bore everyone with a defensive rearguard. I like to play attacking football and that is how we shall play the game tonight." West Ham beat Bury 10-0. Jim's after-match comments were unprintable.

KEN BROWN

One of the most popular players to play for West Ham was centre-half Ken Brown. He came to West Ham in October 1951 from local side Neville United, making his league debut at Rotherham United in February 1953. Being understudy to club captain Malcolm Allison, he was not able to gain a regular place in the team until the 1957/58 season. That year, he won a divisional Championship medal, as the Hammers came top of the Second Division. He played in 41 games that season, and was ever-present during the following campaign, as the Hammers finished in a respectable sixth position in the First Division. This level of consistency in his game won him an England cap, against Northern Ireland at Wembley in November 1959. Sadly, this was to be his only appearance for his country, but glory at club level was soon to follow. Ken was in the West Ham teams that won the FA Cup in 1964, and a year later the European Cup Winners Cup. In 1967, he was awarded a testimonial game, when an All Star XI provided the opposition. When his Hammers career came to an end, he had played in a total of 455 games for the club. He then joined Torquay United, making 53 appearances in two seasons, playing alongside another former Hammer, John Bond. After retiring as a player, he went into management at Norwich City, leading them to a League Cup Final victory against Sunderland in 1985. He was dismissed by Norwich in 1987, and took up the manager's job at Plymouth Argyle until 1991. Ken is one of the nicest men in football, and always shares a smile and a joke with everyone who is fortunate to be in his company. Today, he is a director of a leisure centre near Norwich.

DEBUT DOUBLE

Don Travis scored four goals on his debut for both the reserves and the first team. He scored four against Chelsea reserves in September 1945, and a further four in his first-team debut, against Plymouth Argyle in February 1946; in the same game, winger Terry Woodgate scored a hat-trick in seven minutes. West Ham won 7-0.

HANDBOOK HOWLERS

Back in the 1920s players were not described as they would be today. Here are some extracts from the West Ham handbooks of the time:

Season 1920/21: Frank Burton: Has a long reach of leg, which finds some extraordinary positions. Alf Lee: He is better on wet grounds than hard. James McCrae: Not as proficient at feeding with the ball as he might be.

Season 1921/22: Vic Watson: Rather despondent at times but he will get over it. Stephen Smith: Is not yet quick enough for the first team.

Season 1924/25: Albert Cadwell: Was heard to speak at least three words on the journey to Leeds. Albert Fletcher: Not as fast as we could wish.

Season 1925/26: George Kay: He has spent the summer studying the offside rule.

FRANK O'FARRELL

Frank O'Farrell was a wing-half who came to West Ham in January 1948 from Cork United. He played in over fifty reserve team games before finally making his debut for the first team against Notts County in November 1950. He became a regular for six seasons, playing in 197 league games and 13 FA Cup ties. While at West Ham, he won seven international caps for the Republic of Ireland. Frank was transferred to Preston North End in November 1956 in an exchange deal with Eddie Lewis. Going straight into the side, he scored on his debut against Manchester City. Preston were then in the First Division, and he played in 17 games before he was on the losing side. He played for North End until April 1961, making 129 appearances, many of them as club captain. Retiring as a player in 1961, he became manager at Weymouth, whom he guided to the Southern League title in 1965. That won him the manager's position at Torquay United, after which he took charge at First Division Leicester City. In his first season at Filbert Street, there was some success as runners-up in the FA Cup Final, but there was also disappointment, as Leicester were relegated. However, in 1971 he led them back as Second Division champions. Frank then became boss at Manchester United, but only lasted a year in that position before taking up a similar post at Cardiff City. Another year later, he was on his travels again, this time as manager of the Iranian national team. He rejoined Torquay in 1981 for a spell before his final job in football, scouting work for Bolton Wanderers and Everton. Frank retired in 1993, and now lives happily with his wife in Torquay.

WARTIME CAPS

During the Second World War, international matches were classed as unofficial. Three West Ham players made appearances in these matches:

Ted Fenton for England .... v Wales
Len Goulden for England ....v Wales (3 times) Scotland (3 times)
Archie Macaulay for Scotland ....v England (5 times)

COTTEE ENDS FOREST JINX

Tony Cottee scored at Nottingham Forest in March 1984. In ten successive visits to the City Ground, West Ham had failed to score. Geoff Hurst had been the last to score there, back in 1969.

STATS EXTRA

Up to the end of the 2006/07 season, West Ham had played in 3,376 League fixtures, 310 FA Cup ties, 184 League Cup matches, and 42 games in Europe. In these matches, 601 players appeared. There were 5067 league goals scored, which includes 122 own goals from opponents.

UP FOR THE CUP I

West Ham finished as Second Division champions in 1980/81. They also played in Europe, and reached the League Cup Final. Their League Cup run ended in two games against Liverpool in the final, with the Hammers falling just short.

Stage	Opponents	Outcome
Second round first leg	Burnley (a)	2-0
Second round second leg	Burnley (h)	4-0
Third round	Charlton Athletic (a)	2-1
Fourth round	Barnsley (h)	2-1
Quarter-final	Tottenham Hotspur (h)	1-0
Semi-final first leg	Coventry City (a)	2-3
Semi-final second leg	Coventry City (h)	2-0
Final	Liverpool (Wembley)	1-1
Final replay	Liverpool (Villa Park)	1-2

The Hammers team in the final was: Phil Parkes, Ray Stewart, Frank Lampard, Billy Bonds, Alvin Martin, Alan Devonshire, Jimmy Neighbour, Paul Goddard, David Cross, Trevor Brooking, Geoff Pike. Substitute in both games was Stuart Pearson.

DISMAY IN BELGIUM

After winning the FA Cup in 1975, West Ham played in the European Cup Winners Cup. They reached the final, where the Hammers went down 4-2 to Anderlecht in a thrilling game played at the Heysel Stadium in Brussels.

Stage	Opponents	Outcome
First round	Lahden Reipas (Finland) (a)	2-2
First round	Lahden Reipas (Finland) (h)	3-0
Second round	Ararat Erevan (Soviet Union) (a)	1-1
Second round	Ararat Erevan (Soviet Union) (h)	3-1
Quarter-final	Den Haag (Holland) (a)	2-4
Quarter-final	Den Haag (Holland) (h)	3-1
Semi-final	Eintracht Frankfurt (Germany) (a)	1-2
Semi-final	Eintracht Frankfurt (Germany) (h)	3-1
Final	Anderlecht (Belgium)	2-4

In the final, despite goals from Pat Holland and Keith Robson, West Ham were beaten 4-2, with the team being: Mervyn Day, Keith Coleman, Frank Lampard, Billy Bonds, Tommy Taylor, Pat Holland, Graham Paddon, Billy Jennings, Trevor Brooking, Keith Robson. One of the Anderlecht scorers was Francois Van Der Elst, who was to join West Ham in 1981.

THEY ONLY SCORED ONCE

Here are ten players who made over 100 league appearances, but only scored one league goal:

Player	Apps	Goal Scored
Charlie Bicknell	137	v Plymouth Argyle (h) 1946
Eddie Bovington	138	v Nottingham Forest (h) 1966
Paul Brush	151	v Queens Park Rangers (h) 1985
Albert Cadwell	272	v Newcastle United (a) 1932
George Carter	136	v Leeds United (a) 1921
Alf Chalkley	188	v Manchester City (h) 1932
John Charles	118	v Manchester United (h) 1967
Steve Forde	170	v Bury (h) 1948
Steve Potts	399	v Hull City (h) 1990
Jack Yeomanson	106	v Plymouth Argyle (h) 1948

EIGHT'S GREAT

Between 1990 and 1997, West Ham played Leicester City in eight league games – and won them all.

CONSECUTIVE SCORING RECORDS

In season 1964/65, West Ham scored at least once in each of their first 23 league games. Starting with a 2-1 victory at Fulham on 22 August, they scored in every match up to the 3-0 win at Chelsea on 28 November. The run was ended on 5 December against Leicester City, when an inspired display from Gordon Banks in goal gave his side a 0-0 draw. The club record for consecutive scoring in league games is 27, set in 1957/58 when winning the league. Strangely, when they were relegated in season 1931/32, there was a run of 26 consecutive scoring games.

UPS AND THE DOWNS

The Hammers have enjoyed the euphoria of promotion on six occasions and have suffered the despair of relegation five times:

Promotion	Position	W	D	L	F	A
1922/23	2nd	20	11	11	63	38
1957/58	1st	23	11	8	101	54
1980/81	1st	28	10	4	79	29
1990/91	2nd	24	15	7	60	34
1993/93	2nd	26	10	10	81	41
2004/05	6th	21	10	15	66	56

Relegation	Position	W	D	L	F	A
1931/32	Bottom of 22	12	7	23	62	107
1977/78	20th	12	8	22	52	69
1988/89	19th	10	8	20	37	62
1991/92	Bottom of 22	9	11	22	37	59
2002/03	18th	10	12	16	42	59

ARNOLD HILLS

Arnold Hills was the owner of Thames Ironworks. In his day he was a keen sportsman, and had been English mile champion. He was also a good footballer, having played for Oxford against Cambridge in the annual varsity match, and represented England against Scotland in 1879 while playing for Old Harrovians. He was keen to look after his workers, and when it was suggested to him that a football team be formed, he was delighted, and keen for it to succeed. In those early days, it was Hills' money that was made available to buy players. He also spent considerably when he helped fund the building of the Memorial Grounds in 1897. Arnold Hills died in 1927 at his home in Penhurst, Kent. Without this great man, West Ham United would surely not exist today.

WHATEVER HAPPENED TO THE 1964 FA CUP WINNERS?

Jim Standen: He later played for Millwall and Portsmouth, and ran two sports shops. Jim emigrated to the United States in 1980. There, he worked for a car leasing firm until his retirement. Now happily living in California near to his sons, daughter and grandchildren.

John Bond: He went into management, and became chief at Torquay United, AFC Bournemouth, Norwich City, Manchester City, Burnley, Swansea City, Birmingham City and Shrewsbury Town. John is now retired and living in the Manchester area.

Jack Burkett: He played for Charlton Athletic before becoming player-manager of the Irish side St Patricks Athletic. He later coached Southend United and Fulham. Now living in retirement in Leigh-On-Sea in Essex.

Eddie Bovington: He ran a trio of successful clothes shops in North London, and now keeps fit by being a member of Woodford Green Athletics club, near his home in Epping in Essex.

Ken Brown: He went on to play for Torquay United and Hereford United, and was assistant manager at AFC Bournemouth and Norwich City, before taking over as Norwich manager, later taking a similar role at Plymouth Argyle. He is now a director of a leisure centre near Norwich.

Bobby Moore: At the end of one of the greatest careers in the history of English football, Bobby joined Fulham in March 1974, and played against West Ham in the 1975 FA Cup Final. He later managed Oxford City and Southend United, and worked for Capital Gold, but tragically died in February 1993.

Peter Brabrook: He joined Leyton Orient in July 1968, and later played for Romford, before taking up coaching with a number of local non-league sides. Peter then managed West Ham's under-17 side until his retirement in 2002.

Ronnie Boyce: He joined the Hammers' coaching staff before being appointed chief scout, a job he filled until leaving Upton Park in 1995. Ronnie now lives in a village in Norfolk.

Johnny Byrne: He moved first to Crystal Palace, and then on to Fulham, before emigrating to South Africa, where he managed Durban City and Hellenic. Johnny sadly died in October 1999.

Geoff Hurst: Went on to England glory, and eventually moved to Stoke City, finishing his playing career with West Bromwich Albion and Telford United. He managed Chelsea between 1979 and 1981, and was later a director of a motor insurance company. More recently, he has been involved with promotion work at Upton Park on match days.

Johnny Sissons: Johnny left West Ham to play for Sheffield Wednesday, and later Chelsea. For the past 30 years, he has been living in South Africa, where he is a partner in a motor products company.

SPIRALLING TRANSFER FEES

Very few transfer fees were disclosed until the 1960s, but they've headed ever upwards – from a few hundred pounds to the millions transferred in today's transactions.

Player	From	Year	Fee
Ted Hufton	Sheffield United	1919	£350
Jimmy Andrews	Dundee	1951	£4750
Phil Woosnam	Leyton Orient	1959	£30,000
Johnny Byrne	Crystal Palace	1962	£65,000
Phil Parkes	Queens Park Rangers	1979	£565,000
John Hartson	Arsenal	1997	£3.5m
Marc Vivien Foe	Lens	1999	£4.5m
Tomas Repka	Fiorentina	2001	£5m
Don Hutchison	Sunderland	2001	£5m
Dean Ashton	Norwich City	2005	£7.25m
Craig Bellamy	Liverpool	2007	£7.5m

Player	To	Year	Fee
Danny Shea	Blackburn Rovers	1913	£2,000
Syd Puddefoot	Falkirk	1922	£5,000
Lawrie Leslie	Stoke City	1963	£15,000
Paul Allen	Tottenham Hotspur	1985	£425,000
Tony Cottee	Everton	1988	£2m
John Hartson	Wimbledon	1999	£7.5m
Rio Ferdinand	Leeds United	2000	£18m

FORGOTTEN CAPS

At the end of the First World War, England played four international matches which were known as Victory Internationals. Syd Puddefoot played twice against Scotland and once against Wales. He was England's top goalscorer with four goals.

LONDON A-Z

Looking through the London street guide, you will find many names with a West Ham connection:

West Ham .... Hammers Lane NW7, Boleyn Road E7, West Ham Lane E15
The Managers.................................... Greenwood Drive E4, Lyall Avenue SE21
World Cup Trio............ Moore Road SE19, Peters Lane EC1, Hurst Road E17
Old Favourites............................ Brooking Road E7, Devonshire Drive SE 10
Goalkeepers .... Walker Close SE18, Carroll Close E15, Green Street E13

Plus from the 2006/07 season squad, there's: Collins Street SE3, Noble Court E1, Ferdinand Street NW1, Mullins Path SW14, Harewood Avenue NW1, Parker Street E16 and Ashton Street E14.

WARTIME SHORTAGE

It wasn't only food in short supply during the war, but also footballers. The Hammers arrived a man short for the match at Fulham in December 1940. J Osborne, a Romford player, was due to make his Fulham debut but it was decided that he would play for West Ham instead. The home officials were not too happy when he scored West Ham's winning goal! A few weeks later, both Millwall and West Ham were a man short for their match in the London War Cup. Bill Voisey, the home side trainer, played for the Lions, but the Hammers waited until half-time for Ted Fenton to turn up. In September 1940 West Ham played the entire game with Clapton Orient with only ten men. The extra handicap did not matter much, as the teams drew 3-3. In December 1944, Queens Park Rangers turned up at Upton Park with only nine men. West Ham lent them Ernie Gregory and Reg Attwell, and beat the West Londoners 4-2.

NOT A GOOD WELCOME BACK

After leaving West Ham, the following players came back and scored against the Hammers at Upton Park:

Martin Peters .... for Tottenham Hotspur in December 1974
Paul Ince .... for Manchester United in February 1993
Tony Cottee... for Leicester City in May 1998
Rio Ferdinand.. for Leeds United in April 2000
Frank Lampard...................................... for Chelsea in January 2006
Svetoslav Todorov .... for Portsmouth in March 2006
Jermain Defoe .... for Tottenham Hotspur in May 2006

EX-PLAYER XI

Here is a team of former Hammers now currently playing elsewhere:

David James	Portsmouth
Glen Johnson	Chelsea
Chris Cohen	Nottingham Forest
Carl Fletcher	Crystal Palace
Rio Ferdinand	Manchester United
Michael Carrick	Manchester United
Yossi Benayoun	Liverpool
Frank Lampard	Chelsea
Marlon Harewood	Aston Villa
Jermain Defoe	Tottenham Hotspur
Joe Cole	Chelsea

Manager: Harry Redknapp (Portsmouth)

ACTION REPLAY V

7 November 1966 .... West Ham 7 Leeds United 0 .... League Cup

After just two minutes, the Hammers were in the lead, Byrne slipping the ball to Sissons, who scored. Sissons did the trick again on 24 minutes, finishing off a pass from Brabrook, and the same pair linked once more ten minutes later for Sissons to claim his hat-trick. A shot from Byrne on 41 minutes came off a defender to leave Hurst with a simple goal and the Hammers four goals to the good. On 59 minutes, Byrne found Hurst with a brilliant pass, and the England star drove home a low shot. Another England hero got in on the act twenty minutes later, Peters dribbling past two defenders to send a shot crashing past Harvey in the Leeds goal. Two minutes later Brabrook headed on to Hurst, who completed his hat-trick – a brilliant exhibition of football from West Ham which left Leeds shellshocked. The team on that memorable night was: Jim Standen, Eddie Bovington, John Charles, Martin Peters, Ken Brown, Bobby Moore, Peter Brabrook, Ronnie Boyce, Johnny Byrne, Geoff Hurst, John Sissons.

BOND SCHEME

In 1991, the club needed to raise capital to develop the ground. They introduced a bond scheme – with holders only given the right to purchase a season ticket. Not happy, fans organised boycotts and protests during games. None of this helped matters on the field at a time when West Ham were fighting relegation, but protests forced the club to alter their plans.

NICKNAMES

There have been many Hammers nicknames over the years, and here's a selection of the more choice ones:

Ronnie Boyce	Ticker
Ray Stewart	Tonka
Johnny Byrne	Budgie
Alvin Martin	Stretch
David Cross	Psycho
Bryan Robson	Pop
Paul Goddard	Sarge
John Bond	Muffin
Julian Dicks	Terminator
Martin Allen	Mad Dog

SUMMER TOUR: USA 1969

The Hammers, then managed by Ron Greenwood, embarked on a month-long end-of-season tour in May 1969. The trip involved travelling around the States, covering some 20,000 miles and using six different airlines. Eighteen players made the trip, which involved playing two games against four other British clubs on a league basis - called the International League.

Opponents	Venue	Result
Wolverhampton Wanderers	Baltimore	3-2
Wolverhampton Wanderers	Kansas City	2-4
Kilmarnock	Seattle	1-2
Dundee United	Baltimore	6-1
Aston Villa	Atlanta	2-2
Dundee United	Dallas	3-1
Aston Villa	Baltimore	2-0
Kilmarnock	Baltimore	4-1

West Ham finished runners-up in the league, which was won by Wolverhampton Wanderers. They also played two exhibition matches while away, but both ended in defeat. They were against Tottenham Hotspur, in Baltimore – the game was lost 3-4 – and against Southampton – which was played in Bermuda, where Southampton triumphed 4-2. Players making the trip were: Peter Bennett, Clyde Best, Billy Bonds, Ron Boyce, Trevor Brooking, John Charles, John Cushley, Bobby Ferguson, Trevor Hartley, Paul Heffer, Bobby Howe, Geoff Hurst, Jimmy Lindsay, Bobby Moore, Martin Peters, Harry Redknapp, John Sissons, Alan Stephenson.

GOING UP II

1990/91 was a good season for the club, as they reached the FA Cup semi-final and gained promotion to the First Division. They started the season well, going undefeated in their first 21 league games. On the last day of the season, West Ham were denied the Championship after losing at home to Notts County. Top scorer was Trevor Morley, with 12 league goals. The biggest win came against Hull City, who were beaten 7-1.

Football League Second Division 1922/33

	W	D	L	F	A	Pts
Oldham Athletic	25	13	8	83	53	88
West Ham	24	15	7	60	34	87
Sheffield Wednesday	22	16	8	80	51	82
Notts County	23	11	12	76	55	80
Millwall	20	13	13	70	51	73
Brighton & Hove Albion	21	7	18	63	69	70
Middlesbrough	20	9	17	66	47	69
Barnsley	19	12	15	63	48	69
Bristol City	20	7	19	68	71	67
Oxford United	14	19	13	69	66	61
Newcastle United	14	17	15	49	56	59
Wolverhampton W	13	19	14	63	63	58
Bristol Rovers	15	13	18	56	59	58
Ipswich Town	13	18	15	60	68	57
Port Vale	15	12	19	56	64	57
Charlton Athletic	13	17	16	57	61	56
Portsmouth	14	11	21	58	70	53
Plymouth Argyle	12	17	17	54	68	53
Blackburn Rovers	14	10	22	51	66	52
Watford	12	15	19	59	59	51
Swindon Town	12	14	20	73	73	50
Leicester City	14	8	24	60	83	50
West Bromwich Albion	10	18	18	52	61	48
Hull City	10	15	21	57	85	45

TEN-GOAL RECORD HOLDERS.

When Bobby Zamora was at Brighton & Hove Albion, he scored a goal in ten successive appearances in season 2001/02. Jermain Defoe scored in ten successive league games, while on loan to Bournemouth in 2000/01. Vic Watson achieved the feat for West Ham in season 1924/25. All three finished the season as top goalscorer.

WHO WOULD BE A FOOTBALL MANAGER?

The West Ham Statisticians Group was formed in 1980. A monthly newsletter were sent to members from November 1980 until August 1987, and in July 1985 the club manager John Lyall provided the following article for the newsletter:

A week in the life of a football manager. 22 April to 27 April 1985.

I can fully understand football supporters wondering what a manager actually does between each game and how fully he is involved in the activities of his club. In this day and age we read much of the modern manager not being involved in training, not being involved in the administration of the football side of the club, continually going off to recharge the batteries. I can assure you that this is not the case, and over the years I have noted that the great majority of managers, coaches etc are simply hard-working people. My week is typical of the effort offered at most football clubs throughout Britain, although the content is controlled by the individual.

Monday begins at the training ground at 9am with a discussion about Saturday's performance with my staff. Our normal chats last about an hour and the content is varied: training session to be prepared, form of individual players, analysis of future opposition. At 10.30am we trained for over two hours with the senior players, which involved the correction of problems from the Sunderland match, together with certain physical and technical practices. After lunch my staff and I "patterned out" our training schedules for the week with obvious emphasis on Luton Town. I returned home at 4pm and left again to attend a Youth Cup Final at Upton Park versus Brighton at 5.15pm, with the preparation for the game done by our youth manager Tony Carr. I have the opportunity to talk to the scouts and parents prior to the game which is an important factor as the youth development section of the club is the future. Having drawn the match 2-2 we felt it necessary to discuss the team's performance, and we spoke to the young players for 45 minutes after the match with reference to their strengths and weaknesses. I returned home at 11pm.

Today, Tuesday is a day off for the players and I am spending this morning dealing with any correspondence and various other administration problems. Fortunately I have a highly efficient aide, Mrs Moss who takes much of the time-consuming work from me. This afternoon I will return to the training ground for a reserve game and then come back to Upton Park for a board meeting which will finish around 8.30pm. Tomorrow we will be training in the morning with the senior players and in the afternoon as per usual my staff and I will work with the youth players on their individual techniques. In the evening I intend to watch the Luton game in preparation for our own game with them on Saturday.

Thursday brings a trip to Holland to watch a couple of players who have been recommended to us by our contacts on the Continent. These trips are always worthwhile not only to watch individuals but also to observe and note the tactics and new innovations of the continental football. My chief representative Eddie Bailey always accompanies me on these visits as he logs our comments and opinions and can offer much useful information when we make our comparisons with a similar British player.

We will return on the first flight Friday morning and travel directly to the training ground for our final preparations for Saturday's game with Luton. The morning will involve training, a team meeting involving discussions and debate and of course the selection of all our teams for Saturday's fixtures. In the afternoon I return to Upton Park and made an effort to be home at 5pm. I usually try to spend the evening relaxing at home as I always believe the night prior to a game should be used to "charge the batteries".

On Saturday morning I usually relax and try to arrive at Upton Park around midday. This gives me time to deal with any emergencies and also to make tests on any injured players with our physio Rob Jenkins. And so to the game, a win we hope. Following the match I meet the Press and usually see myself leaving the ground around 7.30 in the evening.

As you will be aware the week is fairly busy but if you read the detail you will be aware of the great variety of stimulation involved in my weekly routine. As I stated earlier this is typical of the involvement of football people and I'm certain few would alter their lifestyle for the conventional nine till five.

FIND IT ON E-BAY

In recent years, more items of memorabilia are being traded on E-bay. There are some bargains to obtain, but some are very costly. Here are some West Ham items that have been up for grabs over the past year:

Programme	Arsenal v West Ham, April 1943	£32
Programme	Brentford v West Ham, January 1944	£54
Programme	West Ham v Leyton Orient, May 1963	£54
Programme	West Ham v Sheffield United, November 1930	£150
Ticket	West Ham v Fiorentina, November 1975	£40
Ticket	West Ham v West Bromwich Albion, January 1967	£25
Handbook	1958 edition signed by 35 players	£90

WELSH WONDERS

The Hammers have not had too many Welshmen playing for them, but this eleven all won international caps for Wales:

Bill Jones 1901/02
Dick Richards..............................1922/23
Wilf James....................................1930-32
Phil Woosnam..............................1958-62
Mark Bowen..................................1996/97
John Hartson................................1996-99
Andy Melville...............................2002-04
Carl Fletcher.................................2004-06
Gavin Williams 2004/05
Danny Gabbidon 2005-
James Collins.................................2005-

MINOR CUP COMPETITIONS

In season 1986/87, a new cup competition for First and Second Division sides, called the Full Members Cup, was introduced into the football calendar. The Hammers played one game in this competition, a 2-1 home defeat to Chelsea. It was replaced by the Simod Cup a year later, and West Ham were beaten 2-1 by Millwall. In 1988/99, the Hammers fared a bit better, beating West Bromwich Albion 5-2 at Upton Park, only to lose to Watford in the next round. For season 1989/90 the competition became known as the Zenith Data Systems Cup the Hammers beat Plymouth Argyle 5-2 at home, but then lost 4-3 at Chelsea. West Ham played their last game in the competition in December 1990, losing 5-1 at Luton Town. All the games had been poorly attended, with the highest gate being the 12,140 who braved the initial match with Millwall.

BORN ON A MATCH DAY

Six players from the 2006/07 season squad were born on a match day. Teddy Sheringham: 2 April 1966 – on this day, West Ham drew 1-1 with Burnley at Upton Park. Marlon Harewood: 25 August 1979 – the Hammers beat Oldham Athletic 1-0 at home. Yossi Benayoun: 5 May 1980 – Charlton Athletic were beaten 4-1 at Upton Park. Nigel Reo-Coker: 14 May 1984 – West Ham lost 1-0 at home to Everton, in what was Trevor Brooking's last game for the club. Carlton Cole: 12 November 1983 – the Hammers won 3-0 away to Wolverhampton Wanderers. Lee Bowyer: 3 January 1977 – the day of a 0-0 draw at home to West Bromwich Albion.

QUALITY HOTEL

When the new Dr Martens Stand was built in 2001, a revolutionary feature was a hotel, with 72 rooms that are converted from Executive Boxes. Each room overlooks the pitch.

FIRST FOOTBALL LEAGUE SEASON

West Ham were elected to the Football League Second Division in 1919. Their first game was a dull 1-1 draw with Lincoln City at Upton Park, with Jimmy Moyes, a Scot signed from Dundee, scoring. A 7-0 defeat at Barnsley was next, but the defence eventually settled down, and proved one of the most stubborn in the division. At home they had a good record, finishing the season with six successive wins at the Boleyn. Notable wins came against Nottingham Forest (5-1), and 4-0 over Wolverhampton Wanderers. Finishing in the respectable position of seventh in their first league season was a good achievement. Syd Puddefoot was top goalscorer with 21 goals, including a hat-trick against Port Vale and four against Nottingham Forest.

Football League Second Division 1919/20

	W	D	L	F	A	Pts
Tottenham Hotspur	32	6	4	102	32	70
Huddersfield Town	28	8	6	97	38	64
Birmingham City	24	8	10	85	34	56
Blackpool	21	10	11	65	47	52
Bury	20	8	14	60	44	48
Fulham	19	9	14	61	50	47
West Ham	19	9	14	47	40	47
Bristol City	13	17	12	46	43	43
South Shields	15	12	15	58	48	42
Stoke City	18	6	18	60	54	42
Hull City	18	6	18	78	72	42
Barnsley	15	10	17	61	55	40
Port Vale	16	8	18	59	62	40
Leicester City	15	10	17	41	61	40
Clapton Orient	16	6	20	51	59	38
Stockport County	14	9	19	52	61	37
Rotherham County	13	8	21	51	83	34
Nottingham Forest	11	9	22	43	73	31
Wolverhampton W	10	10	22	56	80	30
Coventry City	9	11	22	35	73	29
Lincoln City	9	9	24	44	101	27
Grimsby Town	10	5	27	34	75	25

CLEVER TREVOR

Sir Trevor Brooking has had two spells in charge of the team. He did an amazing job, losing just one game out of 14 played. Trevor's full record is:

2002/03

Manchester City (a) 1-0
Chelsea (h) 1-0
Birmingham City (a) 2-2

2003/04

Bradford City (h) 1-0
Ipswich Town (a) 2-1
Reading (h) 1-0
Crewe Alexandra (a) 3-0
Gillingham (a) 0-2
Cardiff City (a) 3-2
Millwall (h) 1-1
Crystal Palace (h) 3-0
Derby County (a) 1-0
Norwich City (h) 1-1
Burnley (h) 2-2

ERNIE GREGORY

Goalkeeper Ernie Gregory gave great service to the club, spending 51 years with them as player and coach. He joined the groundstaff in 1936, and played for the reserves until war broke out in 1939. In between serving in the Essex Regiment and the RAF, Ernie played in 66 regional games, sharing the jersey with Harry Medhurst and George Taylor. He finally made his league debut in December 1946, against Plymouth Argyle at Upton Park. Until 1959, he was a regular in the side, apart from season 1954/55 when he was missing through injury. Honours that came his way included an England B cap against France in 1952 and a Second Division Championship medal in 1958. After playing in 406 games, he retired as a player in 1959. The club awarded him a testimonial in 1960, when the Costa Rican side LDA provided the opposition. After this he became a coach to the reserve team, and later the first team, passing on his considerable experience. Ernie officially retired in May 1987, and the Football League presented him with a long-service statuette. Living locally in Ilford, Ernie still attends matches, and is always pleased to be recognised and sign autographs.

LEAGUE CHAMPIONSHIP WINNERS

There are ten men who've won the Championship after leaving West Ham:

Danny Shea with Blackburn Rovers 1914
Eric Parsons with Chelsea 1955
Ray Houghton with Liverpool.............................. 1988, 1990
Paul Ince with Manchester United........................ 1993, 1994
Tony Gale with Blackburn Rovers 1995
Rio Ferdinand with Manchester United 2003, 2007
Joe Cole with Chelsea 2005, 2006
Frank Lampard with Chelsea 2005, 2006
Glen Johnson with Chelsea.................................... 2005, 2006
Michael Carrick with Manchester United....................... 2007

THE GENIUS OF PAOLO DI CANIO

The Italian midfield maestro was one of the finest players to have worn the claret and blue. Here's a selection of some of his amazing strikes:

Versus Wimbledon, March 2000: Arguably the best goal ever seen at Upton Park. It started with Foe in midfield, who passed out wide to Sinclair. He put over a cross, and Di Canio, in mid air, sent a spectacular right-footed volley into the far corner of the net. The goal won the Goal of the Season award.

Versus Arsenal, October 1999: He flicked the ball over Keown with his left foot before clipping a brilliant 15-yarder into the top corner with his right instep.

Versus Derby County, December 1999: He collected the ball from Minto before bending and dipping a 12-yarder under the right-hand angle.

Versus Chelsea, September 2002: Paolo turned past a defender, scooped the ball up with his right foot, and let fly with a venomous left-footed volley.

Versus Coventry City, April 2000: He took Carrick's pass in his stride, side-stepped Burrows, and cracked in a low 30-yarder which flew in off a post.

FULL ENGLISH

In 2005/06, 42 of West Ham's 52 Premiership goals were scored by English players – the highest total at any Premiership club that season. Meanwhile, Teddy Sheringham became the first outfield player over the age of 40 to play in the Premiership.

HAMMERS NEVER SIGN FOR ARSENAL

The following Arsenal players were all transferred directly to West Ham. However, there has not been a single instance of a West Ham player who left to join Arsenal:

Stan Earle	1924
John Hartson	1996
Jim Marshall	1934
John Radford	1976
Stewart Robson	1986
Davor Suker	2000
Charlie Walker	1936
Nigel Winterburn	2000
Ian Wright	1998

OUR BELOVED CAPTAIN

On 28 June 1993, at Westminster Abbey, a Service of Thanksgiving was held for the life of Bobby Moore. Among the two thousand mourners were the 1966 World Cup-winning side, and legends George Best, Billy Wright and Franz Beckenbauer. Of the Royal family Prince Edward, Prince Philip, and The Duke and Duchess of Kent were present. The Dean of Westminster began by giving the following address: "We meet in this house of prayer to thank God for all his gifts, and especially the qualities and talents which he bestowed on Bobby Moore. We entrust him to God's unfailing mercy, love and forgiveness; and we pray for those who mourn him. For many years, he delighted supporters of West Ham, and was a formidable opponent in the eyes of those against whom he played in the League and FA Cup. But it is for his appearances for England - ninety of them as captain - that he will chiefly be remembered, and supremely for his captaincy of the World Cup team of 1966. So today let us reflect on Bobby Moore's achievement, which stands as a symbol of all that is best in sport; the patient development of an innate ability, a thorough understanding of tactics and teamwork, and a relationship of mutual respect with those against whom he competed. We remember also the kindness and humour which marked his private life, and his loyalty and generosity to his family; the dignity which he maintained in public and in private, and the courage with which he faced death."

HIGHBURY HIGH

West Ham will go down in history as the last team to have beaten Arsenal at Highbury, following their 3-2 victory in February 2006. They were also the first team to beat Arsenal at the Emirates Stadium, 1-0 in April 2007.

LEN GOULDEN

Inside-forward Len Goulden was one of the finest attackers in the country in his day. He joined West Ham in 1931, and made his league debut at the Valley against Charlton Athletic in April 1933. For the next six seasons Len was a regular in the West Ham side, scoring 54 league goals in his 239 appearances up to 1939. During that time, he also gained international recognition, winning 14 England caps – and was in the national side that were infamously forced to give the Nazi salute before a 6-3 victory in Germany. During the War he was in the team that won the League Cup in 1940, and also turned out as a guest for London rivals Chelsea. This led to him moving to Stamford Bridge in 1946, and he played for the Blues until 1950, making 111 appearances and scoring 19 goals. He later coached Chelsea before being appointed manager of Watford in November 1952, staying at Vicarage Road until 1956. Len later coached in Libya, and on returning home he managed Banbury Town and coached Oxford United. He retired to live in Cornwall, and died in 1995.

UNSUNG ACADEMY HERO

West Ham is regarded throughout football as the original youth academy, and for 33 years, youth team manager Tony Carr has been producing players who have gone on to play for the first team. Incredibly successful, he has overseen over sixty graduates from the youth squad. Many have gone on to play for England at some level. Here are a few of those players:

Paul Allen
Michael Carrick
Joe Cole
Tony Cottee
Alan Curbishley
Jermain Defoe
Anton Ferdinand
Rio Ferdinand
Ray Houghton
Paul Ince
Glen Johnson
Kevin Keen
Frank Lampard jnr
Alvin Martin
George Parris
Geoff Pike
Steve Potts
Stuart Slater

CLUB SURNAMES

Thames Ironworks had a player named Sunderland, but since the club changed its name to West Ham United there have been at least four players with surnames the same as other Football League clubs:

Fred Blackburn	1905 to 1912
Alan Blackburn	1954 to 1957
Billy Charlton	1922 to 1923
Archie Hull	1925 to 1928

UNIQUE HAT-TRICKS

In April 1986, West Ham beat Newcastle United 8-1 – and Hammers defender Alvin Martin managed a rather unique treble: each of his three goals came against a different Newcastle goalkeeper. He netted his first against Martin Thomas after three minutes, then beat Chris Hedworth after 64 minutes, before a penalty struck past Peter Beardsley in the 84th minute rounded off his hat-trick. In 1948, Jack Dodds of Lincoln City scored a hat-trick against three different West Ham goalkeepers. The Hammers lost 4-3 to City; and the Hammers goalkeepers who conceded the goals on the day were Ernie Gregory, George Dick, and Tommy Moroney.

FAMOUS FANS

Older Hammers will remember the episode of Til Death Do Us Part in which Alf Garnett, played by Warren Mitchell, spent the game pitchside in a wheelchair, only to dance down the touchline when the Hammers scored late on. Over the years, there have plenty of other famous personalities who have supported the Hammers; here are a few more of them:

Nick Berry	actor
Frank Bruno	boxer
Todd Carty	actor
John Cleese	actor
Noel Edmonds	TV presenter
David Essex	musician
Graham Gooch	cricket
Steve Harris	musician
Lennox Lewis	boxer
Glenn Murphy	actor
Ray Winstone	actor

CHARITY MATCHES

Various Charity games have been played at Upton Park:

31 Jan 1943..RAF v National Police
in aid of the RAF Benevolent Fund

1 May 1958..........................Showbiz XI v Boxers and Jockeys
in aid of the Sportsman's Aid Society

17 Apr 1961....................Ex-West Ham XI v TV Entertainers
in aid of Greater London Fund for the blind

AUTHOR'S DREAM TEAM

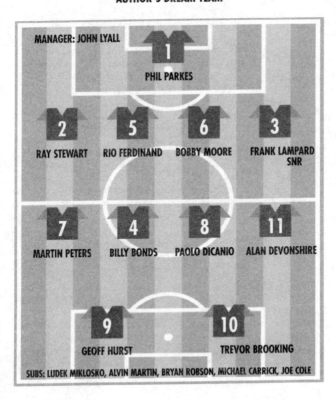

MANAGER: JOHN LYALL

1 PHIL PARKES

2 RAY STEWART — 5 RIO FERDINAND — 6 BOBBY MOORE — 3 FRANK LAMPARD SNR

7 MARTIN PETERS — 4 BILLY BONDS — 8 PAOLO DICANIO — 11 ALAN DEVONSHIRE

9 GEOFF HURST — 10 TREVOR BROOKING

SUBS: LUDEK MIKLOSKO, ALVIN MARTIN, BRYAN ROBSON, MICHAEL CARRICK, JOE COLE

CONTINENTAL TOURS

During the 1920s, West Ham embarked on several summer tours to Europe. With no aeroplanes, and just boats, coaches and trains to travel through Europe, the players were often away for weeks at a time:

1921 Spain

Madrid 4-0
Vigo... 4-0
Bilbao 2-0
Corunna 1-0

1923 Austria and Hungary

Slavia 3-1
Hakoah.. 1-1
Buda 3-2
Sparta 1-1

1924 Germany, Switzerland and France

Cologne... 2-0
Gladbach... 6-1
Mannheim.. 4-0
Frankfurt 4-1
Friburg... 2-5
Berne 1-0
French National team............................. 1-2

1925 Holland

Ajax 2-0
Vitesse 2-3
Swallows 1-1

1925 Spain

Spanish national team 2-1
Real Madrid 2-3
Corunna... 3-0
Corunna... 2-1
Vigo... 2-1
Vigo... 2-3

1927 Denmark, Sweden and Norway

Copenhagen 5-1
Copenhagen 3-0
Copenhagen 2-0
Gothenberg 4-3
Oslo... 6-2

1928 Germany

Eintracht.. 2-1
Nuremburg.. 3-2
Bayern Munich.................................... 2-3
Hertha Berlin 4-2

THAT'S ZAMORA

Bobby Zamora's four play-off goals in 2005 not only helped the Hammers return
to the Premiership, but also inspired a song about him sung by West End musical
singer Mark Adams, and released on CD single. The song That's Zamora is a
re-working of Dean Martin's famous That's Amore. Brighton fans sang a slightly
different version during his time there, but the lyrics to single are:

At Upton Park Academy
The greatest fans will always say

When the ball hits the net, who's the scorer I bet
That's Zamora
With a left foot so sweet, got the world at his feet
That's Zamora

West Ham sing Ting a ling a ling
As they're blowing their bubbles
When we play Tippy tippy tay
That's the end of our troubles

When the Upton Park roar who's the man who will score
That's Zamora
We've got Teddy and Matt always on the attack in our team
Marlon, Thomas and Chris
Anton's hair you can't miss, Reo-Coker
Scuse me but you see back at West Ham F.C
That's Zamora.

1923 FA CUP FINAL CHAOS

It was estimated that up to 200,000 spectators got into the ground that day, and the game was delayed sparking national news headlines:

CUP FINAL CHAOS THAT WAS NEARLY A DISASTER

STADIUM GATES STORMED BY 100,000 PEOPLE

DOCTORS TREAT CLOSE ON 1000 CASUALTIES

BROKEN LIMBS AND SERIOUS INJURIES

ARENA SWEPT BY HUMAN AVALANCHE

The following extract, taken from the following morning's *The Sunday Pictorial* gives a fascinating insight into what went on:

'Little less than a miracle averted disaster on a big scale yesterday at the first Football Cup Final to be played in the arena of the new stadium in the British Exhibition grounds at Wembley. There was room for 127,000 people. Actually over 200,000 got into the ground during a wild rush in which all control went to the winds, barricades were swept aside, and the police were reduced to impotence. Later after the turnstiles had been closed great masses of humanity converged on the Stadium by road and rail at the rate of a thousand per minute. It was a surging throng which could not be held back. There was a big push, the gates were rushed by some 100,000 people, the impact carried many thousands on to the playing pitch, which was soon completely overrun, and the crowd became unmanageable. It was a scene of utter confusion. People stood in their thousands in the middle of the pitch, and the goalposts just overtopped their heads. The lines of play were quite invisible. Organisation had been overwhelmed. The police were helpless. For 40 minutes the pitch was in possession of the invading hordes. Then police reinforcements arrived from Scotland Yard and at last the game began. There was an interruption of nearly a quarter of an hour when the crowd burst through the touchline cordon but after that the game was played to a finish.

THE KING'S ACTION

'It was at a critical moment in a very ugly situation that the King arrived. Truly it was deplorable for him to find that the largest sports ground in the world was not big enough to hold the largest football crowd that had ever gathered. Still amid all the pandemonium the King has never had a finer reception. Every hat was raised. And there was a mighty sound as the vast concourse sang "God Save The King" which was followed by three tremendous cheers. The players pushed themselves through, and appealed to all around them for a chance to play. By and by the players were mobbed, and could neither get in nor out. By slowly maintained pushing and backing by the police horses the pitch, finally, was cleared and at 3.43 the seemingly impossible happened and Vic Watson kicked off for West Ham. But the trouble was not over. Play had been in progress only thirteen minutes when the crowd broke onto the pitch again just in front of the principal stand. Groups of fainting men were laid out near the penalty area and were attended by the ambulance men. Once more the mounted police got busy. The slow task of moving back the people little by little was eventually successful and play was resumed.

MANY WOMEN CRUSHED

'Marvellous indeed is the fact that there was no fatality. Nearly a thousand people were treated by the first aid detachment during and after the match. Many of them were suffering from minor injuries, but there were quite a number of broken legs and collar bones, and serious eye injuries, while there were hundreds of fainting cases. Sixty persons in all were sent to various hospitals. A number of women were badly crushed against the railings. The ambulance men experienced much difficulty in attending to the cases as the gangways became impassable for stretchers.One man had to sit for two hours with a broken shoulder because the Red Cross could not get through the crush.'

ENGLAND HAT-TRICKS

Geoff Hurst .... v West Germany 1966
Geoff Hurst ....v France 1969
Johnny Byrne .... v Portugal 1964

HE DID THE LOT

In 2003/04, the youth player Chris Cohen had a unique experience. The youth team members acted as ball boys at home games. Chris carried out this task; he also played for the U17s, U19s, reserves, and finally the first team... all in one season. He was also called up by England to play in their Under-17 side. He made his first-team debut against Sunderland aged 16, and was the youngest player to appear for West Ham in over 80 years.

THINGS THEY SAID III

In 1995, Tony Cottee wrote in his biography:

'I've got to be honest, one day it would be a dream come true if I became the manager of West Ham and complete my eventful journey from the terraces to the dressing room and on to the manager's office.'

Sadly, his dream will probably not come true after he was involved in a possible takeover of the club announced in April 2005. The board immediately banned him as matchday host and barred him from writing in the club's magazine.

LONDON CHALLENGE CUP

West Ham competed in this competition from 1908/09 until 1973/74. Up until 1946 it was regarded as a first-team competition but after that West Ham fielded mostly a reserve line up. The Hammers reached the Final on 14 occasions, winning it nine times, as follows:

1925	v Clapton Orient 2-1
1926	v Arsenal 2-1
1930	v Brentford 2-1
1947	v Crystal Palace 3-2
1949	v Chelsea 2-1
1953	v Brentford 2-1
1957	v Millwall 3-1
1968	v Dagenham 3-1
1969	v Tottenham Hotspur 3-2

Bobby Moore played in a losing Final against Arsenal in 1958, while Jimmy Barrett and Malcolm Musgrove scored a hat-trick each against Fulham in 1954 in a 9-1 victory in the semi-final.

THINGS THEY SAID IV

In 1984, Ron Greenwood wrote in his biography:

'In 1966 I made an offer to buy goalkeeper Bobby Ferguson from Kilmarnock. Before the deal went through, Matt Gillies the Leicester manager rang to say that Gordon Banks was for sale and that he wanted to come to West Ham. As I had given my word to Kilmarnock I declined his offer. I did what I thought was right and honesty should matter. Hindsight tells me that was one of the biggest mistakes in my life.'

LEAGUE'S FIRST SUB

Keith Peacock, assistant manager to Alan Curbishley in 2006/07, was the first-ever substitute in the Football League. He came on for Charlton during their game with Bolton Wanderers on 21 August 1965.

THEY CAME TOO LATE

Two of the greatest goalscorers in English history signed for West Ham. But sadly they came too late in their careers to make a significant difference Their illustrious careers were spent with London rivals. In addition to their domestic totals, Jimmy Greaves scored 44 goals for England, while Ian Wright hit nine for his country.

Jimmy Greaves's clubs	*Lge Gls*	*FAC Gls*	*LC Gls*	*Euro Gls*
Chelsea	124	3	2	3
Tottenham Hotspur	93	21	5	9
West Ham	13	-	-	-

Ian Wright's clubs	*Lge Gls*	*FAC Gls*	*LC Gls*	*Euro Gls*
Crystal Palace	89	3	9	-
Arsenal	128	12	29	16
West Ham	9	-	-	-

Two other legends who joined West Ham late in their careers were Liam Brady and Paulo Futre. Brady played in 293 league and cup games for Arsenal before playing for Italian sides Juventus, Sampdoria, Inter Milan and Ascoli. While at West Ham he played in 115 games, scoring ten goals. Futre, who came to the Hammers in 1996, had played for some of the world's leading clubs – Benfica, Sorting Lisbon, Real Madrid, Atletico Madrid, Olympique Marseille and AC Milan. Sadly he was past his best at Upton Park and in his short spell he only played in nine league games.

PETER SHILTON

He was one of England's finest goalkeepers, winning 125 caps. He also played in 1005 league games, 87 FA Cup matches, 102 League Cup ties and 24 games in Europe – an amazing career that spanned 32 seasons. Peter spent two years at West Ham from 1995 to 1997 but never made a first-team appearance. He made his Hammers 'debut' on the substitutes bench against Leeds United on 15 January 1996 He played his first game for the reserves against Norwich City at Upton Park on 8 February 1996 and his last appearance was against Brighton and Hove Albion in November 1996. In all he played in ten reserve games before joining Leyton Orient.

MINOR CUPS AND TOURNAMENTS

Anglo Italian Cup Winners Cup: As cup winners in 1975 the Hammers played the Italian team Fiorentina on a home and away basis. West Ham lost 1-0 on both occasions

Watney Cup: This was Britain's first commercially-sponsored tournament. West Ham drew 1-1 with Bristol Rovers at Eastville in August 1973. The resultant penalty shoot out saw the Hammers lose 5-4.

Makita Tournament: This took place at Arsenal's Highbury in August 1991. West Ham were outclassed by Sampdoria from Italy, losing 6-1, and then drew 1-1 with the Greek team Panathinakos, but lost 3-2 on penalties.

Anglo Italian Cup: In 1992, to qualify to play the Italian teams West Ham had to win their English group. This they did by drawing 2-2 at home to Bristol Rovers and beating Southend United 3-0 away. They then proceeded to play four Italian sides but failed to reach the Wembley Final:

Cremonese (a)	0-2
Reggiana (h)	2-0
Cozenza (a)	1-0
Pisa (h)	0-0

Full Members Cup: Open only to First and Second Division sides, the name of the cup changed to the Simod Cup and later the Zenith Data Systems Cup, as each sponsor took over. It was of little interest to fans; the largest gate at Upton Park was 12,140 for the opening match with Chelsea.

1986 Full Members	Chelsea (h)	1-2
1987 Simod Cup	Millwall (h)	1-2
1988 Simod Cup	West Bromwich Albion (h)	5-2
	Watford (a)	1-1*
1989 Zenith Data Systems Cup	Plymouth Argyle (h)	5-2
	Chelsea (a)	3-4
1990 Zenith Data Systems Cup	Luton Town (a)	1-5

* lost on penalties 1-3

Texaco Cup: Another sponsored tournament played in 1974.

Orient (h)	1-0
Luton Town (h)	1-2
Southampton (a)	0-2

Aberdeen Tournament: This was a friendly competition played at Aberdeen's ground Pittodrie in 1981.

Aberdeen 0-3
Manchester United................................ 1-0

Tennent Caledonian Cup: A tournament sponsored by the brewing giant and played in Glasgow at Ibrox in 1979.

Glasgow Rangers 2-3
Brighton and Hove Albion 1-3

GAMES AT UPTON PARK

West Ham played their first game at Upton Park on 1 September 1904 and at the end of the 2006/07 season had played a total of 2409 home games:

Southern League.................................... 208
Football League/Premiership............. 1689
FA Cup.. 144
League Cup 97
European Cup Winners Cup 14
UEFA Cup 3
Intertoto Cup 3
Full Members Cup 1
Simod Cup.. 2
Zenith Data Systems Cup....................... 3
War Years League 1915-1918................. 74
War Years League 1939-1946.............. 113
War Years Cup 1939-1946..................... 26
Anglo Italian Cup Winners Cup............. 1
Anglo Italian Cup.................................... 3
Texaco Cup 2
Essex Professional Cup 12
Southern Floodlight Cup 12
Play Offs... 2

OWN GOALS

Beware own goals when playing Stockport! In a home FA Cup game in 1935 West Ham were leading 1-0 with a minute left when Jim Barrett headed past keeper Herman Conway to give County a shock draw. The replay was lost 1-0. In 1996, the Hammers were 1-0 up in a League Cup tie at County when Iain Dowie headed past Ludek Miklosko. West Ham went on to lose 2-1.

FIRST-EVER MATCH AT UPTON PARK

1 September 1904..*West Ham 3 Millwall 0*

Never has such a scene been witnessed in this district as that which was enacted on the new West Ham ground at Upton Park on Thursday evening. The day was not only the opening of the football season but the formal opening of the club's headquarters. The match booked for the day was fortunately a good one, not only was it a Southern League fixture, but it was Millwall who were to be their opponents. It had been rumoured that West Ham had this year "new blood of sterling quality" with them, so it is to be wondered that 10,000 spectators gathered to watch this match. Smiling faces were to be seen on every side when the players entered the field, and Councillor Anstead, of East Ham set the ball rolling. The homesters were at once on the ball, and pressed to such an extent that in the first three or four minutes Bridgeman was able to net the ball. Then there was a scene, thousands cheered, hats were waved, and many were the cries of "Good old Bridgeman". The " new blood" had apparently worked a miracle for West Ham last season it was expected that they would have dropped out. Even at the outset of this game it was evident that they would not only hold their own but beat their opponents from over the water. West Ham after this score still played a determined game, excellent passing, crisp kicking, contriving to make their supporters happy. The ball which had found its way to the West Ham goal, was beautifully fisted out by Kingsley. The backs got it, it was cleared, then came the turn of the halves. They took their task well. The ball was neatly sent to the forwards by Allison and it was secured by Flynn. He centred, and Bridgeman waiting put in a stinging shot. This caught the crossbar amid loud thundering cheers for Bridgeman's attempt to score. The ball which had rebounded into play was met by Simmons, and placed nicely over to the other wing and them McCartney made a brilliant endeavour to score, failing to find the net by only a few inches. Plenty of good work by both teams shortly afterwards resulted, but most of it was in favour of the homesters, their forwards doing really excellent with the ball. Bridgeman put in a number of creditable shots, but Millwall's goalie was equal on each occasion to the work given him. Half time arrived with West Ham winning 1-0. On resuming Millwall were seen to advantage, and made rapid strides to the home goal. Kingsley was there, however, and he received quite an ovation when he made a capital save. Then West Ham responded to the call of its supporters. The ball was taken to the visitors goal, and Simmons was responsible for a lovely shot, which was saved by Joyce. The Hammers were not to be baulked, for they still combined excellently together, the visitors getting but little of the play. After this brilliant display by the homesters, Bamlett unfortunately kicked one of the visitors men, and a foul being given, Millwall got away. It was indeed fortunate that West Ham had such an excellent custodian, for the shot by

Graham was of the stinging variety. It was cleared by Kingsley in a very smart manner. West Ham were then seen to be playing a winning game, and their front rank deserve every praise for their gallant efforts to score. At last they were rewarded. Flynn centred in fine style, and Bridgeman was then able to net the ball. Then was witnessed what will probably be marked with a white stone in the annals of West Ham football. Directly the ball was kicked off the Hammers got away, and for full two minutes the goal of the visitors was bombarded, but the goalie was equal to the occasion. The ball was cleared time after time by him, but each time it was sent back to him by one or other of the forwards. After a while, it was only for a second or two, Millwall got away, a good grounder was put in by one of the forwards, but once again Kingsley showed his sterling value. The shot was cleared, and the Hammers were off, and in less than it takes to write Flynn had notched their third point. They were not however, satisfied and right to the end endeavoured to score but the posts could not be found. However Millwall could not score and West Ham were contented. They had won by three to nil, and surely they were satisfied. West Ham United: Kingsley, Bamlett, Gardner, Allison, Piercy, Russell, McCartney, Fletcher, Bridgeman, Simmons, Flynn. Millwall: Joyce, Stevenson, McLaren, Blythe, McLean, Baker, Watkins, Jones, Graham, Hunter, Bradbury.

*Source: East Ham Echo

CLEAN SHEETS

The club record for consecutive clean sheets is six. Phil Parkes was the goalkeeper throughout the August 1980 run, when four league games and two League Cup ties were played without conceding a goal. Parkes had a marvellous season in 1980/81, as he kept a clean sheet in 22 league games and seven cup ties in various competitions. The record for consecutive clean sheets in league games is five, which has been achieved on three occasions – first in 1922/23, when Ted Hufton was in goal, followed by Phil Parkes in 1980/81, and Ludek Miklosko ten seasons later.

GOALSCORING PARTNERSHIPS

Three great partnerships which brought plenty of goals were: John Dick and Vic Keeble, who in seasons 1957/58 and 1958/59 between them they scored 87 league goals; Geoff Hurst and Johnny Byrne had their best seasons in 1963/64 and 1964/65 when they scored 80 league goals; while Tony Cottee and Frank McAvennie managed to score 75 league goals in seasons 1985/86 and 1986/87.

GEORGE FOREMAN

He scored one goal in his six league appearances in season 1938/39. A modest total, but what is overlooked is his tremendous rate of scoring throughout the war years. Between 1939 and 1945 he scored 154 league goals and 34 cup goals. This included four goals against Tottenham and Southend in 1940 and four against Aldershot in 1945. He also scored seven hat-tricks, as follows:

1939/40	Portsmouth
	Millwall
1940/41	Queens Park Rangers
1941/42	Brighton
	Chelsea
	Watford
1942/43	Brighton

He also played during the war as a guest player for Tottenham Hotspur where he scored 21 goals taking his total goals scored to an amazing 209.

SCORED WITH A BROKEN LEG

In 1975 during an FA Cup tie at Southampton Bobby Gould played the last half hour of the first half in agony. He scored in that period – but came off at half-time and discovered that his leg was broken.

ALMOST CHAMPIONS

1985/86 was a marvellous season for West Ham, who in finishing third gained their highest-ever placing in Division One. The season started badly with only one win in the first five games. New signing Frank McAvennie, however, had scored a brace against both Queens Park Rangers and Liverpool to give clear warning of his intentions. The Hammers then went 18 successive league games without defeat until they lost by a single goal at Tottenham on Boxing Day. The run included a victory over the champions Everton, five successive away wins and four goals against Aston Villa, Nottingham Forest and West Bromwich Albion. There was one defeat in the period, this being a 1-0 reverse against Manchester United in the League Cup. Tony Gale and Alvin Martin were forming a brilliant partnership at the back. Alan Devonshire was back to his best after nearly two years out of the game, and new signing Mark Ward added to West Ham's tougher approach with his non-stop running and tackling. Both strikers Tony Cottee and Frank McAvennie were scoring regularly as the Hammers approached the New Year. In March morale was low after league games at Arsenal and Aston Villa were lost within one week, vital games which on reflection cost West Ham the title. At Easter further victories over London rivals Chelsea and Tottenham were gained, the 4-0 win at Stamford Bridge being particularly rewarding. But the return clash with Chelsea however brought disappointment as the Blues won 2-1. The Hammers of 1986 were built of stern stuff as they bounced back with a 2-0 victory at Watford. With four home games in only nine days to follow the team needed determination, luck and an injury-free spell. First Newcastle were annihilated 8-1, then came two narrow 1-0 wins against Coventry and Manchester City as both players and fans found the tension unbearable. The final home game of the season saw 31,000 packed into Upton Park and a dramatic late penalty winner from Ray Stewart gave West Ham a 2-1 win over Ipswich Town. On the final Saturday of the season the Hammers won 2-1 at West Bromwich Albion; the celebrations were short-lived as the news came through that Liverpool had won at Chelsea to clinch the championship. The squad had played entertaining football throughout and added a degree of self belief to their game which made them hard to beat.

Football League First Division 1985/86

	W	D	L	F	A	Pts
Liverpool	26	10	6	89	37	88
Everton	26	8	8	87	41	86
West Ham	26	6	10	74	40	84
Manchester United	22	10	10	70	36	76
Sheffield Wednesday	21	10	11	63	54	73
Chelsea	20	11	11	57	56	71
Arsenal	20	9	13	49	47	69
Nottingham Forest	19	11	12	69	53	68
Luton Town	18	12	12	61	44	66
Tottenham Hotspur	19	8	15	74	52	65
Newcastle United	17	12	13	67	72	63
Watford	16	11	15	69	62	59
Queens Park Rangers	15	7	20	53	64	52
Southampton	12	10	20	51	62	46
Manchester City	11	12	19	43	57	45
Aston Villa	10	14	18	51	67	44
Coventry City	11	10	21	48	71	43
Oxford United	10	12	20	62	80	42
Leicester City	10	12	20	54	76	42
Ipswich Town	11	8	23	32	55	41
Birmingham City	8	5	29	30	73	29
West Bromwich Albion	4	12	26	35	89	24

1940 FOOTBALL LEAGUE WAR CUP WINNERS

In 1940, West Ham won the War Cup, by beating Blackburn Rovers 1-0 in the final. Chelsea, Leicester City, Huddersfield Town, Birmingham City and Fulham were beaten to reach the final. The following biographies of the players who played in the Wembley final against Blackburn are taken from the Wembley match programme of June 8 1940.

Herman Conway .... (Goalkeeper)
6ft 0in. 13st. Was the first-team goalkeeper for nearly five seasons before leaving in the Spring of 1939 for Tunbridge Wells Rangers. Had a benefit with West Ham last year. Gladly accepted the invitation to return to the Hammers at the beginning of the war, when all three of the other goalkeepers joined the Army. Conway is a deputy A R P chief in a London district.

Charlie Bicknell .... (Right-back and captain)
5ft 11in. 12st 11lbs. Was born at Chesterfield and went to West Ham from Bradford City in 1936. One of the finest captains the Hammers have ever had. Played in every first-eleven match for two seasons before the war. His cool judgement and enthusiasm claim the admiration of teammates, opponents and supporters alike. Is now a War Reserve Policeman.

Charlie Walker .... (Left-back)
5ft 11in. 12st 4lbs. Was born in Nottingham and joined West Ham from the Arsenal in 1936. Has proved to be one of the best left-backs who has ever worn the West Ham colours. Only missed one first-team game in the 1938/39 season. Is a good tennis player and swimmer. Now works as a draughtsman in an Aircraft Factory.

Ted Fenton ....(Right-half)
5ft 11in. 11st 6lbs. A product of West Ham. Was on the Amateur books for several seasons before signing professional forms. Is now in his tenth season with the club. So far this season he has scored 14 goals. Was honoured by being selected to play in all three games against South Africa in the last close season. Is now a Sergeant-Instructor at the Army Physical Training School.

Dick Walker .... (Centre-half)
6ft 0in. 12st 8lbs. Born at Hackney. Was an Amateur player for West Ham before transferring to Park Royal. Returned to the Hammers as a professional in 1934. On the field he is a very serious and determined player, but off the field is noted for his wit. Is an excellent cricketer but is busy just now as an engineer in an Aircraft factory.

Joe Cockroft.. (Left-half)
5ft 8in. 11st. A Yorkshireman from Barnsley. Was secured from Gainsborough in 1933. A skilful half-back, a great tackler and a glutton for work. Holds the club record for the number of consecutive appearances. A good swimmer. Now engaged in engineering in an Aircraft Factory.

Sam Small .... (Outside-right)
5ft 9in. 11st 5 lbs. Born at Birmingham and transferred from Birmingham City in 1937, and is thus in his fourth season as a Hammer. An unselfish type of player who gives a wholehearted ninety minutes for his club in every game. Has scored fourteen league goals this season. Is a Coach builder by trade and is now building Ambulances.

Archie Macaulay ....(Inside-right)
5ft 11in. 12st 4lbs. Is a Scot from Falkirk. Before he donned West Ham colours in 1937 he was with Glasgow Rangers. A clever player of true Scottish type, and deadly in front of goal. A wholehearted player with a great personality. Now a sergeant in the Essex Regiment.

George Foreman .... (Centre-forward)
5ft 9in. 12st 6lbs. A local product who joined West Ham from Walthamstow Avenue towards the end of last season. Was then one of the most outstanding amateur players. Possesses the ideal build for the centre position, and is a good shot. Has scored thirty-five goals in league games for West Ham this season. Is now engaged as an Aircraft Engineer.

Len Goulden... (Inside-left)
5ft 9in. 10st 2lbs. Another local lad who has made good. Now in his eighth season as a Hammer. Holds fourteen International, two League and three trial Caps. Is a cricketer of County standard. Like so many of his colleagues he is now working in an Aircraft Factory.

Stan Foxall... (Outside-left)
5ft 11in. 11st. Born in Lincolnshire. Went to West Ham from the Gainsborough club. Was a dental student before becoming a professional footballer. Has a remarkable turn of speed and a most unorthodox style which often not only leaves his opponents, but also his team-mates guessing. Has scored fifteen league goals this season.

HARRY'S OWN GOAL

When Bournemouth faced Manchester United in the League Cup in 1982, amidst an injury crisis, they drafted in coach Harry Redknapp who had not played for five years; he scored an own goal after 28 minutes.

EIGHT-GOAL THRILLER

One of the highlights for West Ham fans is when the Hammers beat Tottenham Hotspur. When the Spurs came to Upton Park on 6 November 1976 the Hammers were second to bottom in the league and badly needed a win. After 20 minutes West Ham went ahead when Pop Robson was on hand to convert a Brooking free-kick. Five minutes later it was Brooking again as he crossed for Billy Bonds to head home. In the second half Spurs pulled one back when Duncan headed home a cross from Taylor. Then Brooking scored his first goal of the season when his cross sailed past Daines in the Tottenham goal. On 69 minutes a good pass from Geoff Pike allowed Billy Jennings to grab the fourth. Three minutes later Alan Curbishley volleyed home the goal of the game from well outside the box. At 5-1 the home crowd were jubilant but this changed. With 12 minutes to go Hoddle rammed home a shot, and Osgood scored from a penalty three minutes later. Amazingly the eight goals scored had been scored by eight different scorers. To the delight of the home faithful, at the end of that season Tottenham were relegated.

THEY FINALLY WORE THE SHIRT

In August 2003 two players achieved a lifetime ambition to play for the team that they supported as boys. Kevin Horlock joined West Ham as a trainee in 1999, but after playing in youth and reserve games he left in 1992 on a free transfer to Swindon Town. He played in 192 league and cup games before being transferred to Manchester City for £1.25m in 1997. He played for the Sky Blues for six seasons playing in 229 matches. He was now an established Northern Ireland International with 32 caps. In August 2003 the midfielder jumped at the opportunity to join the Hammers and was able to go on to make 33 appearances for his boyhood team. Kevin later joined Ipswich Town, playing in 61 matches for them. Robert Lee signed for Charlton Athletic in 1983, after which he played in 331 matches scoring 62 goals. A fee of £700,000 took him to Newcastle United in 1992 where he became an established England International, gaining 21 caps. While with the Magpies he made 353 appearances, scoring 53 goals. Rob then joined Derby County in 2002 and played 50 matches for the Rams before a free transfer brought him home to West Ham. On joining Rob said "Most of my mates are season-ticket holders who have been waiting a long time for me to arrive here." He was now nearing the end of his career and only played in 19 games before a free transfer took him to Oldham Athletic for a non-playing spell. He then signed for Wycombe Wanderers in 2005, where he seemed to take on a new lease of life. It was a shame both players joined West Ham towards the end of their careers; as at their peak both were internationals and quality players.

FRIENDLY MATCHES

Over the years the club have played in hundreds of friendly matches, many of them with mixed elevens to make it difficult to state that it was a first-team friendly. Here are some first-team friendlies played in the 1950s. Testimonial games have not been included. All were played at Upton Park:

1950	Celtic	5-2
1951	Charlton Athletic	1-5
	RS Liege (Belgium)	3-2
1952	Charlton Athletic	3-3
1953	Blackburn Rovers	1-2
	St Mirren	3-3
	Sunderland	2-0
	Hearts	7-0
1954	St Mirren	3-1
	Servette (Switzerland)	5-1
	Olario (Brazil)	0-0
	VFB Stuttgart (Germany)	4-0
	SC Wacker (Austria)	3-1
	AC Milan (Italy)	0-6
1955	Portsmouth	4-1
	Holland SC (Holland)	0-0
	Distillery (Northern Ireland)	7-5
	SK Rapid (Austria)	1-1
1956	Kaiserslautern (Germany)	2-4
1957	Sparta Prague (Czechoslovakia)	3-3
	Sparta Rotterdam (Holland)	5-0
	Lodz (Poland)	4-1
1959	FC Austria (Austria)	2-0
	Dukla Prague (Czechoslovakia)	1-1

THE CLUB BADGE

The basic crossed hammers motif was used on programmes and handbooks from the early 1900s. But it wasn't until the 1950s that it was first seen on the players shirts. In 1968 a new club crest was designed which incorporated the crossed hammers together with a castle emblem. The crossed hammers were derived from the old Thames Ironworks days when the hammers were the symbol of their trade. The castle came from a building which stood next to the ground for many years called Green Street House. The building had turrets, which resembled a castle, and this was incorporated into the badge. The design of the badge was modified in 1999 to produce a more modern appearance.

VICTOR RAILTON

Journalist Vic joined the *Evening News* as a 14-year-old boy and stayed with them for 43 years until his death in March 1978. He was the football editor, a great journalist and a good friend to many managers and players. Although he had to be impartial, he did have a soft spot for the Hammers whom he watched at every opportunity. A memorial match was held at Upton Park on 2 May 1978 between West Ham and a Bobby Moore XI. An entertaining game saw West Ham win 5-4.

HAVE A DRINK ON US

After retiring as players, a few West Ham lads made their living at some time owning or running a pub:

Bill Adams .... Half Way Inn, Chandlers Ford, Hampshire
Jeroen Boere .... Half Moon, Epping, Essex
Fred Cooper .... Essex Arms, Stratford, Essex
Noel Cantwell .... New Inn, March, Cambs
Julian Dicks .... Shepherd & Dog, Langham, Essex
Kevin Lock .... Prince Of Wales, Mountnessing, Essex
Andy Malcolm .... Ship & Anchor, Maldon, Essex
Alan Stephenson.............. Queens Head, Wormingford, Essex

UPTON PARK BLITZED

In the summer of 1944 a German flying bomb exploded on the pitch and demolished a large part of the South Bank terracing and part of the West Stand. The damage caused meant that West Ham had to play their first 14 games all away from home. In this period they had nine successive wins, two draws and only three defeats. They returned to Upton Park for their first home game against Tottenham Hotspur on the 2 December. Playing in Football League South that season West Ham finished as runners up.

INAUGURAL LEAGUE MATCH

Thames Ironworks played their first League game on 19 September 1896 in the London League at home to Vampires. Left-winger George Gresham had the honour of scoring the first-ever league goal in a 3-0 victory. A crowd of 1260 saw the following Thames team appear: Barnes, Stevenson, Hurst, Morton, Dandridge, Davie, Dove, Rossiter, Hatton, Morrison, Gresham. The other two goals were both scored by Edward Hatton. Thames finished as runners-up in the league to the 3rd Grenadier Guards.

THAMES IRONWORKS SHIP BUILDING & ENGINEERING COMPANY LTD

It is well documented that the workers of Thames Ironworks formed a football team which later became West Ham United Football Club – but what is not generally known is that the shipbuilding company was famous throughout the world. From 1846 until the factory closed in 1912 the company had built up to a thousand Battleships, Cruisers and Life Boats. As its peak the shipyard employed over 7000 men, covering an area of 30 acres of buildings and docks at Canning Town. Records show that 144 warships and 287 merchant ships were launched from the yard. In 1860 HMS Warrior was built, being 9137 tons and 380ft long. At the time it was the biggest warship in the world. The Warrior ended her days with the Navy in 1979 – but she is now restored and can be seen by the public in Portsmouth Harbour. A short list of other vessels built by Thames is as follows:

HMS Albion	1898	battleship
HMS Cornwallis	1901	battleship
HMS Duncan	1901	battleship
HMS Thunderer	1911	battleship
HMS Blenheim	1890	cruiser
HMS Grafton	1892	cruiser
HMS Theseus	1892	cruiser
HMS Black Prince	1904	cruiser
HMS Zebra	1895	destroyer
HMS Grampus	1910	destroyer

There was tragedy for the company when the 6000-ton Albion was launched on 21 June 1898. There were around 30,000 spectators present to see the event, but the wooden gantry beside the ship was not built to hold so many people. When the ship was launched the wooden structure snapped, throwing all the people upon it into the muddy waters. Many were pulled from the water – but sadly a total of 38 perished. The Ironworks ran into financial difficulties in 1912 and despite the efforts of its owner Arnold Hills a closure notice was put on the main gates in December 1912. Hills put up his own notice up which read as follows:

Do not let such a notice spoil your Christmas,
The fight is not yet finished and no battle is lost until it is won.
I will not desert you in the darkest hour before dawn,
I bid you be of good cheer.
Our extremity is God's opportunity and I do not doubt,
There is still in store for us a happy new year.

A BYGONE AGE

Look back in time to 1957 and you find an era when the players played for the love of the game and supporters stood happily on the terraces to catch a glimpse of their heroes. Prices were:

Ground 2s 0d (10p)
Enclosure 3/6 (17p)
Seats 6s 0d (30p)
Season Tickets .... £7-00 and £5-00
Four-page programme .... Threepence (2p)

Back then clubs did not start the season with pre season friendlies or a tour. Invariably the first team played the reserves. For their first practice match West Ham put out teams named as 'Club Colours' v 'Blues'. On that sunny day in August 1957 playing for the club colours were John Lyall and a young Bobby Moore. The following Saturday the Club Colours played the Whites before an attendance of 5300. National Service was still in force and it was noted that Brian Rhodes, Harry Obeney and Andy Nelson were still serving in the Army. Floodlights were a new innovation in those days and the club announced that they had agreed with Blackburn Rovers and Sheffield United to play their fixtures at Upton Park under floodlights. After seven games the first team found themselves in 16th place in the Second Division table. Dick Walker, who had played 311 games for the club, was given the proceeds of his testimonial match, which amounted to £1872. A big signing was made when Vic Keeble was bought from Newcastle United for £10,000. A British rail excursion to Rotherham for the next league game was advertised at 22s 0d (£1.10) return. The introduction of Keeble into the side paid off as Huddersfield Town were beaten 5-2 and Stoke City 5-0. By early December, Hammers had climbed the table to fifth. In an FA Youth Cup tie against Chelsea Bobby Moore faced Jimmy Greaves. In the Blackpool line-up for an FA Cup tie in January was the famous Stanley Matthews. A great display by West Ham saw them win 5-1. In the programme notes the crowd were asked to encourage the team by making a roar when they attacked. The timing of the roar, it was said, is much more effective with the approach to the penalty area or when a corner is taken. West Ham went top of the league after scoring six against both Bristol Rovers and Swansea Town, then went goal crazy as Johnny Dick scored four in an 8-0 rout of Rotherham United. In a Southern Junior Cup Final against Arsenal the two West Ham half-backs were Geoff Hurst and Bobby Moore. Little did they know of a much bigger final they would be playing in some eight years later. On the final day of the season West Ham won 3-1 at Middlesborough to become Second Division Champions.

HAMMERS DOWN UNDER

In May 1995 the club embarked to Australia to play a series of friendly matches, which pleased their many fans now living down under. The fans were disappointed to learn that many of the first-team players had been left behind and only a young side was taken. The first match took place on 19 May against Western Australia at Perth's Waca stadium. A 10,000 crowd saw goals from McPherson and Watson give the Hammers a 2-2 draw. There was a penalty shoot-out to decide the game but West Ham lost that 5-3. Playing for the Aussies was winger Stan Lazaridis who later signed for West Ham. A 2000-mile trip to Melbourne followed for a match against Victoria at Olympic Park, on Sunday 21 May. The game ended 1-1 with the Hammers goal being scored by Danny Shipp, before a sparse crowd of 3500. Next up was the Australia under-23 team played on 24 May in the Marconi Stadium in Sydney. Malcolm McPherson scored the only goal of the game in the second half to record their first win. The return with the under-23 team took place on May 27 in Brisbane. The team was weakened as Potts, Breacker and Allen had returned home a few days before the match. The young Australians took full revenge for their earlier defeat by winning 4-0 before a crowd of 6998. The tour had been good experience for youngsters Steve Blaney, Malcolm McPherson and Darren Currie.

UNLUCKY HAMMERS

Two signings promised so much with West Ham unfortunately ended in disappointment. In July 1993 defender Simon Webster arrived from Charlton for £525,000. As Charlton captain, he had played 140 games for Athletic. During pre-season training he suffered a broken leg in a collision with Julian Dicks. The long recovery began but more injuries followed, including a fractured left ankle. He finally got to make his debut by coming on as a sub against Blackburn Rovers at Upton Park in April 1995. He played a further four games that season – all as a substitute – but sadly that was it. He quit to become physio at the club and later took the same position at Gillingham. Another unlucky Hammer was Richard Hall who came from Southampton for £1.9 million in July 1996. Big things were expected of the England Under-21 international centre-back. In a pre-season friendly at Carshalton he picked up a foot injury which put him out action for nine months. He made his debut against Middlesbrough at Upton Park in April 1997 and played in the remaining six games of the season. He did not know it at the time but these seven games were to be the sum total in Hammers colours. Richard then suffered an horrendous two-year period with a toe injury which eventually forced him to retire in May 1999. Injuries are part of the game but it's a shame these two players never got to show the West Ham fans their undoubted talent and determination.

JIMMY GREAVES DEBUT

He made his debut at Manchester City on 21 March 1970 and continued his amazing record of debut goals with two against City in a 5-1 win. The Hammers travelled to Maine Road having won just three of their last 16 matches. On a muddy pitch Greaves predictably opened the scoring by slotting past Joe Corrigan after ten minutes. City equalised through Francis Lee three minutes later, but after that West Ham took control. After 37 minutes a scramble in the City area resulted in Greaves being first to the ball to slide it home. Just before half time Hurst scored with a header for the third goal. In the 83rd minute came an amazing goal from Ronnie Boyce. The city keeper Corrigan took a goal kick that reached the half way line. The ball came to Boyce who on looking up saw an unguarded net and hit a volley which sailed past Corrigan into the goal. It was Ron's first goal in three seasons and turned out to be his last for the club. A couple of minutes from the end Geoff Hurst volleyed a fifth goal to complete a vintage display. Everyone was talking about the goalscoring of Greaves but it was the goal from Ronnie Boyce that is always remembered by the Hammers fans.

CELTIC CONNECTION

Several players have played for both Celtic and West Ham; while Liam Brady was Celtic manager, Steve Walford was assistant boss at Celtic Park.

Eyal Berkovic
Allen McKnight
Frank McAvennie
Stuart Slater
Marc Rieper
Ian Wright
Paolo Di Canio

CLUB MAGAZINE

In October 1981 the club issued a new magazine called *Hammers Monthly*. It provided an in-depth coverage of the club that could not be found in other publications. It was good value at 50p for 40 pages. The first season there were six issues. For season 1982/83 the price increased to 75p but after three issues the magazine ceased publication due to sales figures. In January 1987 a new publication was issued by the club entitled *Hammers News*. This was in the form of a newspaper with 28 pages for 20p. It stayed as a newspaper until August 1994 when under its new look it became an all-colour glossy magazine costing £2 for 48 pages. The magazine has proved popular with the supporters and the issue now has over sixty pages.

CUP UPSETS

Like any other club, West Ham have suffered their share of embarrassing defeats in both the League Cup and FA Cup at the hands of lower-league opponents:

1962	Plymouth Argyle (a) 0-3	FA Cup
1967	Swindon Town (a) 1-3	FA Cup
1969	Mansfield Town (a) 0-3	FA Cup
1971	Blackpool (a) 0-4	FA Cup
1972	Stockport County (a) 1-2	League Cup
1974	Hereford United (a) 1-2	FA Cup
1978	Swindon Town (h) 1-2	League Cup
1979	Newport County (a) 1-2	FA Cup
1987	Barnsley (h) 2-5	League Cup
1989	Torquay United (a) 0-1	FA Cup
1992	Crewe Alexandra (two legs) 0-2	League Cup
1996	Grimsby Town (a) 0-3	FA Cup
1996	Stockport County (a) 1-2	League Cup
1999	Swansea City (a) 0-1	FA Cup
1999	Northampton Town (two legs) 1-2	League Cup
2006	Chesterfield (a) 1-2	League Cup

WESTERN LEAGUE CHAMPIONS

As well as playing in the Southern League, the Hammers competed in the Western League from 1901 until 1909. In season 1906/07 they finished as league winners in the B section. They then played a championship decider against Fulham who had won the A section. The game was played at Stamford Bridge before a crowd of 10,000 who saw West Ham win 1-0. Results for that season were:

Opponents	Home	Away
Plymouth Argyle	6-2	0-3
Portsmouth	3-3	3-2
Tottenham Hotspur	5-0	0-4
Southampton	3-0	1-0
Millwall	1-0	3-0

WEST HAM LADIES

The ladies team was first formed in season 1992/93. Since then they have progressed to and currently play in the FA Premier Womens League South. They also have a reserve side and four junior teams.

FIVE ALIVE AND SIX OF THE BEST

Hammers striker Brian Dear will never forget Good Friday morning 16 April 1965. It was on this day that he scored five goals against West Bromwich Albion at Upton Park. What was incredible was that they were all scored in a 20-minute spell just before and after half-time. Here is how the goals were scored:

Goal One: A minute before the interval Brabrook fed Peters down the right-wing. and his slide rule pass was steered home by Dear.

Goal Two: On 53 minutes Brabrook made a run and passed to Burkett. His centre was headed on to Dear who chested the ball down before crashing it home.

Goal Three: Three minutes later, after a move between Sissons and Peters, Dear hit a shot that slipped through Potter's hands and into the net.

Goal Four: A further three minutes passed and Potter parried Hurst's shot against the post. Dear was on hand to score his fourth.

Goal Five: On 64 minutes Dear completed his quintet, as he was on hand to push home Brabrook's cross.

For the record West Ham won the game 6-1; the other came from Martin Peters. The Hammers team that day was: Jim Standen, Joe Kirkup, Jack Burkett, Martin Peters, Dave Bickles,Bobby Moore, Peter Brabrook, Ronnie Boyce, Geoff Hurst, Brian Dear, John Sissons. Ace marksman Geoff Hurst scored six goals against Sunderland on 19 October 1968 as the Hammers equalled their record league victory of 8-0. A crowd of 24,903 saw Hurst's six-goal haul; the other two came from Bobby Moore and Trevor Brooking.

Goal One: On 18 minutes Peters sprinted through on the right and from his centre Hurst headed home. He later admitted that he had used his hand to score.

Goal Two: Hurst's second goal came from a Trevor Brooking cross in the 34th minute.

Goal Three: A minute before the interval a short corner by Billy Bonds was sent into the middle by Harry Redknapp; Hurst rammed it in at the far post.

Goal Four: Three minutes into the second half Hurst controlled a ball from Martin Peters before cracking it wide of Montgomery.

Goal Five: On 61 minutes a Billy Bonds centre reached Hurst on the edge of the penalty area and he hit a right foot drive.

Goal Six: Ten minutes later Harry Redknapp laid on the ball to Hurst who obliged with his sixth goal.

West Ham lined up as follows: Bobby Ferguson, Billy Bonds, John Charles, Martin Peters, Alan Stephenson, Bobby Moore, Harry Redknapp, Ronnie Boyce, Trevor Brooking, Geoff Hurst, John Sissons.

ONES THAT GOT AWAY

The following three players played for West Ham reserves, and then went on to have excellent careers with other clubs. Bullard and Holland never played a first-team game for West Ham, and Houghton only played for 20 minutes, at Arsenal in May 1982.

Houghton's clubs	Lge Apps	Gls	FAC Apps	Gls	LC Apps	Gls
Fulham	129	16	12	2	4	3
Oxford United	83	10	3	0	13	3
Liverpool	153	28	27	4	14	3
Aston Villa	95	6	7	2	13	2
Crystal Palace	72	7	4	0	6	0
Reading	43	1	4	0	9	0
Total	575	68	57	8	59	11

Holland's clubs	Lge Apps	Gls	FAC Apps	Gls	LC Apps	Gls
Bournemouth	104	18	3	0	6	0
Ipswich Town	259	38	12	0	24	6
Charlton Athletic	126	11	10	1	8	0
Total	489	67	25	1	38	6

Bullard's clubs	Lge Apps	Gls	FAC Apps	Gls	LC Apps	Gls
Peterborough United	66	11	6	1	2	0
Wigan Athletic	145	10	4	0	8	1
Fulham	4	2	0	0	0	0
Total	215	23	10	1	10	1

Glasgow-born Houghton also made 73 international appearances for the Republic of Ireland. Lancashire-born Holland also made 49 international appearances for the Republic of Ireland. Jimmy is currently playing for Fulham. Not bad for three West Ham reserves.

DISMISSALS

In the last ten seasons 45 players have been sent off. It is interesting to note that 29 of them have been on opponents' grounds There have also been 16 sendings off in London Derbies.

1997/98

Steve Lomas	Blackburn Rovers	Away
Samassi Abou	Tottenham Hotspur	Away
John Hartson	Bolton Wanderers	Away
John Hartson	Derby County	Home
Dave Unsworth	Crystal Palace	Away

1998/99

Neil Ruddock	Leeds United	Away
John Moncur	Tottenham Hotspur	Away
Ian Wright	Leeds United	Home
Shaka Hislop	Leeds United	Home
Steve Lomas	Leeds United	Home

1999/2000

John Moncur	Coventry City	Away
Marc Vivien Foe	Arsenal	Home
Shaka Hislop	Middlesbrough	Away
Javier Margas	Chelsea	Away
Steve Lomas	Tottenham Hotspur	Away
Igor Stimac	Chelsea	Home
Trevor Sinclair	Arsenal	Away
Marc Vivien Foe	Leeds United	Home

2000/01

Igor Stimac	Leicester City	Home
Stuart Pearce	Everton	Home

2001/02

Tomas Repka	Middlesbrough	Away
Tomas Repka	Blackburn Rovers	Away
John Moncur	Macclesfield Town	Away
Paolo DiCanio	Chelsea	Away

2002/03

Ian Pearce	Tottenham Hotspur	Away
Tomas Repka	Fulham	Home
Steve Lomas	Arsenal	Away
Fredi Kanoute	Leeds United	Away
Ian Pearce	Bolton Wanderers	Away

2003/04

Jermain Defoe	Gillingham	Away
Jermain Defoe	West Bromwich Albion	Home

Jermain Defoe	Walsall	Away
Mattie Etherington	Norwich City	Away
Steve Bywater	Millwall	Away
David Connolly	Crystal Palace	Away

2004/05

Rufus Brevett	Leicester City	Away
Chris Cohen	Burnley	Home
Steve Lomas	Coventry City	Away
Hayden Mullins	Brighton & Hove Albion	Home
Marlon Harewood	Millwall	Away
Tomas Repka	Preston North End	Home

2005/06

| Paul Konchesky | Newcastle United (Rescinded) | Away |
| Hayden Mullins | Liverpool | Home |

2006/07

| Paul Konchesky | Fulham | Away |
| Bobby Zamora | Fulham | Home |

EARLY CHARITY MATCHES

In 1924 the West Ham directors and players were always aware that there were many less fortunate than themselves. They had a genuine desire to give something back to the community. This led to two charity matches at the end of season 1923/24. The first game was a match against Tottenham Hotspur in aid of the Dockland settlement. The aim of the games was to help provide facilities for young lads to enjoy sport in a deprived area. There was a good response and a crowd of about 10000 turned up – amongst them HRH the Duke of York. Spurs took the lead just before half-time; two minutes from the end West Ham equalised from a penalty taken by Jack Young. The Royal visitor presented both teams with gold medals. The ball was auctioned for the cause and the Hammers chairman William White paid 50 guineas. A month later on Thursday 12 April Scottish giants Celtic provided the opposition for a second friendly match; this was for the benefit of the St Annes Young Men's Club. Former Hammers favourite Syd Puddefoot was a guest in the Celtic line-up. He had earlier been transferred by West Ham to Falkirk. There was a 13,000 crowd to see the Hammers take the lead after three minutes with a headed goal from Viv Gibbins. The visitors equalised through Cassidy during the first half. A few minutes after the interval West Ham went ahead again with a goal from Billy Moore. The Celtic equaliser came from none other than Syd Puddefoot who was pleased no doubt to score against his former team-mates. The game ended all-square and the St Annes Club benefited by some £500.

A TREBLE FOR PARDEW

Alan Pardew played against West Ham for three different clubs. He first played against them for Crystal Palace on 17 September 1991 at Selhurst Park. Ian Wright scored for Palace that day but the Hammers won 3-2. A year later in 1992 he was back at Upton Park playing for Charlton Athletic, who beat West Ham 1-0. It was Alan himself who scored the goal from a pass from Rob Lee who later joined the Hammers. In season 1996/97 West Ham were paired with Barnet in the League Cup. Two legs were played and Alan played in both matches against the Hammers, who eventually won the tie on aggregate by 2-1. While at Barnet, Alan went on loan to Tottenham Hotspur and played in all four of their Intertoto Cup matches in July 1995.

HOUDINI HAMMERS

After West Ham lost 4-3 at home to Tottenham on 3 March 2007 they found themselves bottom of the league, and ten points adrift of safety. With only nine games remaining it seemed inevitable that the Hammers would be relegated. But an amazing turn in fortune followed: and the team put together a run of championship-winning form, winning seven of the final nine games. Defenders Lucas Neill, James Collins and Anton Ferdinand were superb at the back and behind them was the brilliant goalkeeper Robert Green – who put on an amazing display in a 1-0 victory at Arsenal. Up front was Carlos Tevez, credited by many to be the catalyst for the revival. He was inspired in every game, scoring six goals in the incredible run. Going into the final game of the season, against newly-crowned Champions Manchester United, West Ham knew a draw would ensure survival, but defeat could lead to relegation. A dramatic 1-0 win, with Tevez scoring the goal, kept West Ham up at Sheffield United's expense, and earned the team the tag of the 'Houdini Hammers'.

WEST HAM UNITED FOOTBALL CLUB

SEASONAL & PLAYER RECORDS

MISCELLANEOUS SEASONAL RECORDS

Most Total Wins ....28 .... 1980/81
Most Total Draws..............................18 .... 1968/69
Most Total Defeats............................23 .... 1931/32
Most Total Goals Scored............... 101 .... 1957/58
Most Total Goals Conceded .... 107 .... 1931/32

Least Total Wins................................9 .... 1987/88, 1991/92
Least Total Draws..............................4 .... 1934/35, 1964/65, 1982/83
Least Total Defeats ....4 .... 1980/81
Least Total Goals Scored ....35 .... 2006/07
Least Total Goals Conceded.............29 .... 1980/81

Most Home Wins ....19 .... 1980/81
Most Home Draws ....10 .... 1981/82
Most Home Defeats...........................10 .... 1988/89
Most Home Goals Scored.................59 .... 1958/59
Most Home Goals Conceded ....44 .... 1930/31

Least Home Wins ....3 .... 1988/89
Least Home Draws ....1 .... 1934/35, 1980/81
Least Home Defeats...........................1 .... 1957/58, 1980/81
Least Home Goals Scored.................19 .... 1988/89
Least Home Goals Conceded ....11 .... 1920/21, 1922/23

Least Away Wins...............................1 .1925//26, 1932/33, 1937/38, 1960/61
Least Away Draws.............................1 .... 1982/83
Least Away Defeats ....3 .... 1980/81
Least Away Goals Scored ....11 .... 2006/07
Least Away Goals Conceded.............16 .... 1990/91

Most Away Wins...............................11 .... 1922/23, 1957/58
Most Away Draws..............................10 .... 1968/69
Most Away Defeats ....17 .... 1932/33
Most Away Goals Scored ....45 .... 1957/58
Most Away Goals Conceded.............70 .... 1931/32

SOUTHERN LEAGUE 1900-01 TO 1914-15
Full Appearances and Goals Scored

Player	Seasons	League	Goals	FA Cup	Goals
Allan Robert	1900-02	52	1	5	
Allison Tommy	1903-08	156	7	9	
Ambler Charlie	1901-02	1		1	
Ashton Herbert	1908-14	224	23	25	2
Askew William	1912-14	104	2	8	
Atkins C	1908-09	2	1		
Bailey Daniel	1912-14	49	13	4	3
Bamlett Herbert	1904-05	18		1	
Barnes William	1902-03	49	5	5	
Beale Robert	1913-14	1			
Bell George	1911-12	2			
Bigden James	1900-03	91	3	5	
Biggar William	1902-03	8			
Birnie Alexander	1903-04	1		1	
Blackburn Fred	1905-12	217	24	20	4
Blackwood John	1904-05	4	1		
Blythe Joe	1902-03	52		5	
Blyth James	1906-07	3			
Bourne Stanley	1906-07	13		3	
Bourne William	1913-14	1			
Bradford T	1911-12	1			
Brandon Thomas	1913-14	33		3	
Bridgeman Billy	1903-05	72	19	3	1
Brown William	1907-08	20	4		
Brunton Fred	1904-05	1			
Burrill Frank	1911-13	17	2		
Burton Frank	1912-14	50	4	6	
Burton John	1908-09	15	3	4	
Bush Robert	1902-05	20	1	1	
Butchart J	1903-04	3			
Butcher George	1909-14	62	9	9	3
Caldwell Tommy	1909-11	84	12	12	1
Campbell John	1902-03	18	1		
Cannon Frank	1909-10	3	1	1	
Carr James	1914-15	9	1		
Carrick Chris	1904-05	18	6		
Carter Henry	1912-13	10			
Casey Jack	1912-14	74	12	9	1
Caton Harry	1912-14	10			
Chalkley George	1908-09	7		4	

Player	Seasons	League	Goals	FA Cup	Goals
Church William	1903-04	2			
Clarke David	1906-08	17			
Cope Bill	1914-15	31		2	
Corbett Fred	1900-01	33	13	2	2
Costello Frank	1908-09	12	3		
Cotton Charlie	1903-05	18		1	
Craig Charlie	1900-01	53		7	
Curtis Frank	1909-10	6	4		
Davidson Alexander	1902-03	9	2		
Dawson C	1908-09	6			
Dawson Harold	1911-12	22	3		
Denyer Albert	1912-13	46	16	4	1
Denyer Frank	1913-14	2			
Dove Charlie	1900-01	13		3	
Dow James	1902-03	13		1	
Dyer James	1908-09	3			
Earl Arthur	1903-04	1			
Eastwood H	1908-09	6			
Eccles George	1902-03	59		5	
Evans Arthur	1902-03	1			
Fair Aubrey	1902-06	31	1	2	
Fairman Robert	1909-11	90		12	
Farrell John	1902-03	20	3	1	
Featherstone Arthur	1905-07	24	1	1	
Fenton Fred	1900-01	14	2	5	1
Fenwick Alf	1914-15	19	1	2	
Fletcher Jack	1904-05	25	7	1	
Flynn Jack	1904-05	20	3	1	1
Ford William	1905-06	7	1		
Forster Harry	1912-13	40		4	
Foster Jack	1908-09	15	9		
Frost A	1910-11	4			
Frost James	1907-08	20	4	5	
Gardner Dave	1904-06	77		3	
Gault James	1907-08	48		2	
Geggus John	1909-11	31			
Glover Vic	1911-12	29		5	
Goddard J	1913-14	1			
Grassam Billy	1900-08	169	65	10	3
Griffiths Fred	1902-03	48		4	
Hamilton	1904-05	5			
Hammond Syd	1904-07	32		2	
Harrison Fred	1910-12	54	19	8	4

Player	Seasons	League	Goals	FA Cup	Goals
Harwood Alf	1907-08	12			
Haynes Vincent	1909-10	15	5		
Hilsdon George	1904-14	85	31	7	4
Hilsdon Jack	1903-04	1			
Hindle Harry	1905-06	3			
Hitchens J	1901-02	1		1	
Horn George	1906-07	8		1	
Hughes Joseph	1911-14	90		15	
Hunt Fergus	1900-01	42	9	6	1
Ingham William	1903-04	2			
Irvine George	1912-13	21			
Jackson James	1905-06	24			
Jarvis Len	1903-08	133	5	7	
Jenkinson William	1901-02	19	2		
Jones William	1901-02	15			
Kaye Albert	1900-01	14	2	6	3
Kelly William	1900-02	33		4	
Kemp Fred	1906-07	10			
Kennedy William	1910-11	21	10	2	
King Syd	1900-02	59		7	
Kingsley Matt	1904-05	29		1	
Kirby William	1903-04	33	10	3	1
Kitchen George	1905-10	184	5	21	1
Kyle Peter	1901-02	1		2	
Lavery William	1909-10	17		2	
Leafe Alf	1913-14	63	33	6	4
Lee Tom	1907-08	6			
Lindsay David	1906-07	51	4	2	
Linward William	1901-02	40	3	2	1
Lonsdale Thomas	1913-14	21			
Lyon Herbert	1903-04	29	4	4	5
Mackesy Jack	1911-14	10	2		
Mackie Charles	1905-06	10	3		
Mapley Percy	1903-04	13		4	
Massey Frederick	1909-11	38		3	
McAteer T	1902-03	13			
McCartney Alex	1905-06	6			
McCartney William	1904-05	28	3	1	
McDonald Alex	1901-02	4	2		
McEachrane Roderick	1900-01	53	5	7	
McGeorge Robert	1901-02			2	
Mercer Fred	1903-04	7	1		
Miecznikowski W	1902-03	3			

Player	Seasons	League	Goals	FA Cup	Goals
Miellear Joe	1910-11	3		1	
Miller Walter	1908-09	11	5	6	1
Milnes Frederick	1904-05	2		2	
Monteith Hugh	1900-01	53		7	
Moore Tommy	1900-01	4			
Morrison J	1911-12	15	1		
Neil George	1900-01	1			
Oakes William	1903-04	14			
Parkinson Harry	1902-03	2			
Piercy Frank	1904-11	214	7	17	
Pinder	1900-01	1		1	
Pudan Richard	1900-01	7		2	
Puddefoot Syd	1912-14	55	28	6	7
Raisbeck Len	1900-01	2		2	
Randall Tommy	1906-14	189	9	16	1
Ratcliffe George	1900-01	41	14	2	
Redward Frank	1911-12	6		1	
Redwood George	1910-11	4		2	
Reid James	1900-01	13	5	6	
Robertson	1907-08	1			
Rothwell James	1910-13	88	4	11	
Russell John	1904-05	16		1	
Satterthwaite Charlie	1903-04	32	13	4	5
Scanes Albert	1909-10	3	3		
Shea Danny	1907-12	179	111	22	10
Shreeve Fred	1908-10	65	4	10	
Silor William	1909-10	6			
Simmons Charlie	1904-05	34	8	1	
Smith Sidney	1904-05	2	1		
Speak George	1914-15	13			
Stallard Arthur	1913-14	13	8		
Stapley Harry	1905-07	71	39	4	2
Sugden Sidney	1902-03	1			
Taylor Frank	1900-01	12	4	1	1
Taylor Archie	1907-08	59		7	
Taylor William	1906-07	4			
Thompson A	1903-04	9	1		
Tirrell Alf	1913-14	7			
Tirrell Pat	1908-09	13	1	4	
Tranter Wilf	1900-01	4		2	
Tresadern Jack	1913-14	6			
Waggott David	1908-09	10	3	1	
Wagstaffe George	1909-10	3			

Player	Seasons	League	Goals	FA Cup	Goals
Walden George	1911-12	2			
Walker Len	1900-01	1			
Wallace L	1901-02	17	3	1	
Ward T	1901-02			1	
Watson Lionel	1905-07	76	26	4	1
Watts Ernest	1903-04	25	1	4	1
Webb George	1908-11	52	23	10	9
Webster Joe	1914-15	17			
Whiteman Robert	1909-14	136	3	10	
Wildman William	1906-07	39		2	
Wilkinson H	1905-06	14	2	1	
Winterhalder Arthur	1905-06	18	6	2	1
Winterhalder Herbert	1905-06	4			
Woodards Dan	1906-14	109	3	14	
Wright P	1914-15	10	1		
Yenson William	1901-08	50		7	
Young Robert	1907-08	42	1	2	
Own Goals	*All seasons*	4			
TOTALS		5918	793	550	86

FOOTBALL LEAGUE 1919/20 TO 2006/07
Full Appearances and Goals Scored

Player	Played	Lge	Gls	FAC	Gls	LC	Gls	Euro	Gls	PO	Gls
Abou Samassi	1997-98	14+8	5	3+3		2+1	1				
Adams William	1936-37	3	1								
Alexandersson Nic	2003-04	5+3									
Aliadiere Jeremie	2005-06	1+6				+1					
Allen Clive	1991-93	36 +2	17	2+2	1	2					
Allen Martin	1989-95	163+27	25	14	4	15+3	5				
Allen Paul	1979-84	149+3	6	15+3	3	20+4	2	1+1			
Allen Percy	1919-22	80	5								
Allen Robert	1919-20	1	1								
Allison Malcolm	1950-57	238	10	17							
Alves Paolo	1997-98	+4									
Anderson Edwin	1933-34	26		2							
Andrew George	1996-97	2									
Andrews Jimmy	1951-55	114	21	6	1						
Armstrong Eric	1947-48	1									
Arnott John	1953-54	6	2	5							
Ashton Dean	2005-	9+2	3	2	3						
Attreveld Ray	1991-92	1									
Atwell Reg	1937-46	5									
Ayris John	1970-76	41+16	1	1		6+1	1				
Bailey Dan	1919-20	35	9	3	1						

Name	Years						
Baillie David	1925-28	16					
Bainbridge Ken	1946-49	80	16	4	1		
Ball Jack	1929-30	15	9				
Banner Arthur	1938-47	27					
Banton Dale	1979-81	2+3					+1
Barnes Bobby	1980-85	31+12	5	5+1	1	2+2	+1
Barrett Jim	1949-54	85	24	2	1		
Barrett James W	1924-38	442	49	25	4		
Bassila Christian	2000-01	+3		+1			
Beesley Mick	1960-61	2	1				
Bell Richard	1938-39	1	1				
Bellion David	2005-06	2+6				1+1	1+1
Benayoun Yossi	2005-07	55+8	8	7		1	
Bennett Les	1954-55	26	3	2	1		
Bennett Peter	1963-70	38+4	3	2		3	
Berkovic Eyal	1997-98	62+3	10	7+1	2	6	
Best Clyde	1969-75	178+8	47	12	3	20	
Betts Eric	1950-51	3	1				
Bickles David	1963-66	24+1		2		1	
Bicknell Charlie	1935-46	137	1	12			
Biggin Horace	1919-20	2					
Bilic Slaven	1995-96	48	2	1		5	
Bing Doug	1951-54	29	3		4		
Birchenough Frank	1919-20	1					
Bishop Ian	1989-97	240+14	12	22+1	3	21+1	

Player	Played	Lge	Gls	FAC	Gls	LC	Gls	Euro	Gls	PO	Gls
Bishop Syd	1920-26	159	10	13							
Black Robert	1936-37	2									
Blackburn Alan	1954-57	15	3	2							
Blanco Kepo	2006-07	1+7	1					2			
Bloomfield Jimmy	1965-66	9+1		2	1						
Blore Vince	1935-36	9									
Boa Morte Louis	2006-	8+6	1	2		1+1	1	4	1	1	
Boere Jeroen	1993-95	15+10	6	2		13	1				
Bond John	1951-64	381	32	30	1	65+2	6				
Bonds Billy	1967-87	655+8	48	46+2	2			15		3	
Boogers Marco	1995-96	+4						8			
Bovington Eddie	1959-67	138	1	19		18	1				
Bowen Mark	1996-97	15+2	1			3					
Bowyer Lee	2002-	28+2		1				13	2		
Boyce Ronnie	1959-72	275+7	21	20+1	5	23	2				
Boylan Lee	1996-97	+1									
Brabrook Peter	1962-67	167	33	17	3	23	6	7			
Bradshaw Harry	1919-20	14		1							
Brady Liam	1986-89	79+10	9	9	1	14+3				2	
Breacker Tim	1990-98	229+11	8	27+1		20+1				1	
Breen Gary	2002-03	9+5		2		2				1	
Brett Ron	1959-60	12	4	1							
Brevett Rufus	2002-05	24+1	1			4					
Brignull Phil	1978-79	+1									

Player	Years									
Britt Martin	1962-65	20	6			6	1	11+1		
Brooking Trevor	1967-83	521+7	88	40	3	55	8	15		3
Brown Ken	1952-66	386	4	26	1	28				
Brown Kenny	1991-95	55+8	5	7+2		2+1				
Brown Bill	1920-23	60	15	11	5					
Brush Paul	1977-84	144+7	1	17		12+1		1+3		
Bunbury Alex	1922-23	2+2		+1						
Burgess Dick	1922-23	2								
Burkett Jack	1961-67	141+1	4	18	1	17		7		
Burnett Dennis	1965-66	48+2		4		10	2	2		
Burrows David	1993-94	29	1	3		3	1			
Burton Frank	1919-20	64	2	5						
Burton Stan	1938-39	1								
Butcher George	1919-20	34	8	4	2					
Butler Peter	1992-94	70	3	3		4				
Byrne Johnny	1961-66	156	79	18	7	19	15	12	6	
Byrne Shaun	1999-2001	+2				+1				
Bywater Steve	1999-2006	57+2		5						
Cadwell Albert	1923-32	272	1	25						
Calladine John	1920-21	1								
Camara Titi	2000-02	5+6		1+1						
Campbell Greg	1984-85	3+2								
Campbell John	1923-27	28	11	1						
Cantwell Noel	1952-60	248	11	15						
Carole Sebastian	2003-04	+1								3+1

Player	Played	Lge	Gls	FAC	Gls	LC	Gls	Euro	Gls	PO	Gls
Carr Franz	1990-91	1+2									
Carrick Michael	1999-2002	128+8	6	11		8		+1			3
Carroll John	1948-49	5									
Carroll Roy	2005-07	31		2				2			
Carter George	1919-25	136	1	19		1					
Cartwright John	1958-60	4									
Carvalho Dani	1995-96	3+6	2								
Cater Ron	1946-49	63		7							
Chadwick Luke	2004-05	22+10	1	3		1					
Chalkley Alf	1931-36	188	1	14							
Chapman Eddie	1948-49	7	3								
Chapman Lee	1993-94	33+7	7	6	2	4+1	2				
Charles Clive	1971-73	12+2		+1		1					
Charles Gary	1999-2000	2+3						4			
Charles John	1962-69	117+1	1	1		19	1				
Charlton William	1922-23	8									
Chiswick Peter	1953-54	19									
Cisse Edouard	2002-03	18+7		2		1					
Clark Sandy	1982-83	26	7	1		7	3				
Clarke Clive	2005-06	2				1					
Clarke Simon	1990-92	+3									
Cockroft Joe	1932-38	251	3	12							
Cohen Chris	2003-06	2+16		+1		2+1					
Coker Ade	1971-73	9+1	3	1							

Player	Years								
Cole Carlton	2006-	5+12	2	2	1	6+1	1	1+1	
Cole Joe	1998-2002	108+18	10	10+1	2	6	2	2+3	3
Coleman Keith	1973-76	96+5	2	3		2		6+1	
James Collins	2005-	29+1	3	3		2		1	
Collins Jimmy	1923-35	311		25					
Connolly David	2003-04	37+2	10	4	2				
Conway Herman	1934-38	122		5					
Conwell Laurie	1935-36	8	1						
Cooper Fred	1955-57	4							
Cope William	1919-21	106		8					
Corbett David	1936-37	4							
Corbett Norman	1936-49	166	3	8					
Coshall John	1928-29	2							
Cottee Tony	1982-96	266+13	115	29	12	27	18		
Courtois Laurent	2001-2002	5+2				+1			
Cowell Herbert	1920-21	1							
Cowie George	1981-82	6+2				1			
Cowper Peter	1924-25	2							
Cox Charlie	1927-31	89		8					
Coyne Chris	1998-99	+1							
Crawford Ian	1961-62	24	5	1		1	2		
Cross David	1977-81	178+1	77	14		24	12	6	6
Cross Roger	1968-69	5+2	1			1			
Crossley Charlie	1922-23	15	1						
Crowther George	1920-21	3		1					

Player	Played	Lge	Gls	FAC	Gls	LC	Gls	Euro	Gls	PO	Gls
Cumming James	1919-20	15									
Curbishley Alan	1974-78	78+7	5	5		3		1+1		3+2	1
Cushley John	1967-69	38		4		4					
Dailly Christian	2000-	133+25	2	14+6		8	1				
Dare Billy	1954-58	111	44	8	5						
Davenport Calum	2004	15+1									
Dawkins Trevor	1964-66	5+1									
Day Mervyn	1973-78	194		14		14		9			
Deacon Richard	1932-33	3									
Deane Brian	2003-04	9+17	6	3	1				4	+3	
Dear Brian	1962-70	67+2	33	6+1	2	3		6			
Death Steve	1968-69	1									
Defoe Jermain	2000-04	62+31	29	4+1	6	6+1	6				
Dell Fred	1936-37	4									
Devlin Joe	1946-52	70		2							
Devonshire Alan	1976-89	345+13	29	36	1	45+3	2	4	1		
DiCanio Paolo	2000-02	114+4	47	5	1	7	1	10			
Diawara Kaba	1998-2002	6+5									
Dick George	1948-49	14	1	1							
Dick Johnny	1953-62	326	153	21	11	4	2				
Dickens Alan	1982-88	173+19	23	19+3	3	14+3	3				
Dickie Alan	1961-65	12				2					
Dicks Julian	1987-98	262	50	23	3	30	8			1	
Dixon Bob	1928-32	65		3							

Name	Seasons										
Dixon Tommy	1952-54	39	21	3	2						
Dolan Eamonn	1986-89	9+6	3			4					
Donald Warren	1983-84	1+1									
Dowen Jack	1935-36	1									
Dowie Iain	1990-97	70+10	12	3+1	1	10+1	2				
Dowsey John	1926-27	1									
Dumitrescu Ilie	1995-96	5+5		1	1	2+1	1				
Dunmore Dave	1959-60	36	16			2					
Dunn Richard	1946-47	11	2								
Durrell Joe	1971-72	5+1									
Dwyer Noel	1958-59	36		2							
Eadie Doug	1966-67	2									
Earl Alf	1925-32	191	56	15	2						
Earle Stan	1924-31	258		15							
Eastman George	1924-25	2									
Edwards William	1922-25	37	3	2							
England Ernie	1930-31	5									
Ephraim Hogan	2005-	128+6	11	11+1	1	+1		+1		6	1
Etherington Matthew	2003-	1	1			5+1					
Ette Cliff	1933-34	41+2	6	1+1							
Eustace Peter	1969-71	1			1	2+1					
Evans Arthur	1930-31	2									
Fashanu Justin	1989-90	1				+1					
Fenton Ben	1937-38	21	9	1							
Fenton Ted	1932-38	163	18	13							

Player	Played	Lge	Gls	FAC	Gls	LC	Gls	Euro	Gls	PO	Gls
Fenwick Alf	1919-20	2									
Ferdinand Anton	2003-	96+17	3	12		4+1		1		3	1
Ferdinand Les	2002-03	12+2	2					9			
Ferdinand Rio	1995-2000	122+5	2	9		11+1					
Ferguson Bobby	1967-79	240		17		19					
Feuer Ian	1999-2000	3									
Finn Neil	1995-96	1									
Fletcher Bert	1922-23	8	1								
Fletcher Carl	2004-06	32+12	3	4+3		+1					
Foan Albert	1950-56	53	6	7	3						
Foe Marc Vivien	1998-99	38	1	1		3		5+1	1		
Forde Steve	1937-51	170	1	6							
Foreman George	1928-39	6	1	3	1						
Foreman John	1934-36	49	7	2							
Forrest Craig	1997-2000	26+4		4	2	3		1			
Foster Colin	1989-93	88+5	4	9	5	5					
Foxall Stan	1934-38	106	37	7							
Foxe Hayden	2000-01	7+4		+1							
Fryatt Arthur	1930-32	3									
Futre Paulo	1996-97	4+5									
Gabbidon Danny	2005-	49+1	5	8		1					
Gale Tony	1984-93	293+7		29	1	28+2	1			2	
Gall Tommy	1934-35	1									
Gallagher Joe	1982-83	8+1		1		1					

Gamble Fred	1930-31	2	2						
Garcia Richard	2001-05	4+12		+1		+5	12	6		2
Gatland Bill	1920-21	1							
Gazzard Gerry	1949-53	119	29	7	3				
Gibbins Viv	1923-31	129	58	9	5				
Goddard Paul	1980-86	159+11	54	10+1	3	26	3		1
Goodacre Reg	1930-32	20	1						
Gordon Dale	1993-95	8+1	1	+1		1			
Gore Reg	1938-39	5							
Gould Bobby	1973-75	46+5	15	4	1	2			
Goulden Len	1932-38	239	54	14	1				
Greaves Jimmy	1969-70	36+2	13	1		1			
Green Tommy	1919-20	3							
Green Tommy	1936-38	40	6	4					
Green Robert	2006-	26				1			
Green Bill	1976-77	35	1	2		3			
Gregory Ernie	1946-59	382		24					
Gregory John	1951-52	24	6	1					
Grice Mike	1955-60	142	18	7	1				
Grotier Peter	1968-72	50				1			
Guest Joe	1936-37	3	1						
Gunning Harry	1952-53	1							
Gurkin John	1921-22	1							
Hales Derek	1977-78	23+1	10	3	3	4			
Hall Almer	1946-48	50	11	6					

Player	Played	Lge	Gls	FAC	Gls	LC	Gls	Euro	Gls	PO	Gls
Hall Richard	1996-98	7		+1		6	3	1+1			
Hallas Geoff	1954-55	3									
Hampson Tommy	1920-24	70		9							
Harewood Marlon	2003-07	123+19	47	13+1	5					6	1
Harkes John	1995-96	6+5		1+1							
Harley John	2003-04	15	1	1							
Harris Jim	1930-31	7	1								
Hart Joseph	1920-21	1									
Hartley Trevor	1966-68	4+1									
Hartson John	1996-98	59+1	24	7	3	6	6				
Hawkins Bert	1951-52	34	16	3							
Hebden Jack	1920-27	110		6							
Heffer Paul	1966-71	11+4		1+1	1						
Henderson Billy	1921-27	162	7	21	1	6+2					
Hilton Paul	1983-88	47+13	1	4+3		12					
Hislop Shaka	1998-2006	121		14				9		2	
Hodges Harry	1923-24	2									
Hodges Lee	1997-98	+3		+3							
Hodgson Tommy	1921-29	87		5							
Holland Pat	1968-80	227+18	23	12+4	4	22+3	3	10			
Holligan Gavin	1998-99	+1									
Holmes Jim	1936-37	2									
Holmes Mattie	1992-94	63+13	5	6		4					
Hooper Harry	1950-55	119	39	11	5						

Player	Years									
Horler George	1922-27	47		5						
Horlock Kevin	2003-04	23+4	1	4		2				
Houghton Ray	1981-82	+1								
Howe Bobby	1966-71	68+7	4	3		2+2				
Hubbard Cliff	1938-39	1	1							
Huffon Ted	1919-31	371		31						
Hughes Michael	1994-97	76+7	5	7	1	7				
Hughton Chris	1990-91	32+1		7						
Hugo Roger	1963-64	3	2							
Hull Archie	1926-28	2								
Hurst Geoff	1958-71	410+1	180	26	23	47	43	15	2	
Hutchison Don	1994-2005	66+32	16	3+2		5+1	2			+1
Ilic Sasa	1999-2000	1								
Impey Andy	1997-98	25+2		3	1	4				
Ince Paul	1986-89	66+6	7	8+2		9	3			
Inns Tommy	1933-34	4								
Jackman Derek	1948-50	8								
Jackson Tom	1921-22	3								
Jackson Billy	1927-28	2	1							
James David	2000-04	91		6		5				
James Billy	1920-21	54	7	3						
James Wilf	1930-31	40	7	1						
Jennings Sam	1924-25	9	3							
Jennings Billy	1974-79	89+10	34	11	2	3+2		5+2	3	
Johns Stan	1950-51	6	2							

Player	Played	Lge	Gls	FAC	Gls	LC	Gls	Euro	Gls	PO	Gls
Johnson Glen	2002–03	14+1		+1							
Johnson William	1919-20	2									
Johnson William	1926-27	15	7								
Johnson Bill	1932-33	5									
Johnstone Bobby	1956-57	2									
Jones Rob	1999-2000									1	
Jones Steve	1992-96	13+11	4	4+2	1	+1					
Kaine Bill	1924-25	7									
Kane Alex	1925-26	2									
Kanoute Fredi	1999-2003	79+5	29	5	4	3					
Katan Yaniv	2005-06	2+4		+2							
Kay George	1919-25	237	15	22	2						
Kearns Fred	1949-53	43	14	2	1						
Keeble Vic	1957-59	76	45	4	4						
Keen Kevin	1986-92	187+32	21	15+7	1	21+1	5				
Keller Mark	1998-2000	36+8	5			4+1	1	6+1			
Kelly David	1988-89	29+12	7	6		11+3	5				
Kelly Paul	1989-90	+1									
Kilgallon Matt	2003-04	1+2				1					
Kinsell Harry	1950-54	101	2	4							
Kirkaldie Jack	1936-38	11	1	1							
Kirkup Joe	1958-65	165	6	8		7		7			
Kitchener Bill	1966-67	11				1					
Kitson Paul	1996-2001	46+17	18	4+1	1	2+2	1	3+5		2	

Player	Seasons									
Konchesky Paul	2005-06	58+1	1	7	1	1+1		2		
Labant Vladimir	2001-02	7+6		+2						
Lama Bernard	1997-98	12		2			1	15	E	
Lampard ffrank	1967-84	546+5	18	43	2	54	8	10	4	
Lampard Frank jnr	1995-2000	132+16	23	13	2	14+1		10		
Landells Jack	1933-34	21	3	1						
Lane Harry	1919-20	19								
Landsdowne Billy	1978-79	5+4	1			4+1				
Landsdowne Bill	1955-62	57	5	3						
LaRonde Everald	1981-82	6+1				6+1		+1		
Lazaridis Stan	1995-99	53+16	3	9+1			3			
Leafe Richard	1919-21	31	7	1						
Lee Alf	1919-21	26		2						
Lee Robert	2003-04	12+4		+1		2				
Leslie Lawrie	1961-62	57		1		3				
Lewis Eddie	1956-57	31	12	5	3					
Lewis Harry	1935-36	4	4							
Lindsay Jimmy	1968-70	36+3	2	4		2				
Livett Simon	1990-91	1		+1						
Llewellyn David	1969-71	2+4								
Lock Kevin	1971-77	122+10	2	11+1	1	13	2	4		
Lomas Steve	1996-2002	179+8	10	10+3		13		10		3
Loughlin Jim	1927-28	10	4							
Lutton Bertie	1972-73	8+4	1	1						
Lyall John	1958-62	31	2	2		2				

Player	Played	Lge	Gls	FAC	Gls	LC	Gls	Euro	Gls	PO	Gls
Macaulay Archie	1937-46	83	29	7	2						
MacDougall Ted	1972-73	24	5			1					
Mackay Malky	2004-05	17+1	2	3		1					
Mackesy Jack	1919-22	10									
Mackleworth Coiln	1966-67	3									
Malcolm Andy	1953-61	283	4	21		2					
Mangnall Dave	1934-35	35	29	2	1						
Margas Javier	1998-2000	21+3	1			2				2+1	
Marquis Paul	1993-94	+1									
Marsh Mike	1993-94	46+3	1	6	1	6	1				
Marshall Jimmy	1934-36	57	13	2							
Martin Alvin	1977-95	462+7	27	40		71	6	2		6	
Martin Dean	1991-92	1+1		+1							
Martin Tudor	1936-37	11	7								
Mascherano Javier	2006-07	3+2	1								
Matthews Terry	1955-56	9				2					
Mautone Steve	1996-97	1				7					
McAlister Tom	1981-88	85		7							
McAnuff Jobi	2003-04	4+9	1							+1	
McAvennie Frank	1985-91	134+19	49	19+1	6	11+2	2				
McCann Grant	2000-01	+4				1					
McCartney George	2006-	16+6		2		1					
McClenahan Trent	2004-05	+2				1					
McCrae Jimmy	1919-20	50	4								

Player	Years	Lg App	Lg Gls	FAC App	FAC Gls	LC App	LC Gls	Eur App	Eur Gls
McDowell John	1970-78	243+6	8	19		21	1	7	
McGiven Mick	1973-77	46+2	8	3		2		1+1	
McGowan Danny	1948-53	81		2	1	6			
McKnight Alan	1988-90	23		4					
McMahon Pat	1932-33	16		1					
McPherson Keith	1984-85	1				2+3			
McQueen Tommy	1986-89	24+6		1				1	3
Mean Scott	1997-98	+3							
Mears Tyrone	2006-07	3+2							
Medhurst Harry	1938-46	24							
Mellor Neil	2003-04	8+8	2	9		1+1			
Melville Andy	2003-05	14+3		+3		+1			
Miklosko Ludek	1989-97	315		25		25		5	
Miller Keith	1968-69	1+2				+1			
Milne Ralph	1989-90								
Mills Hugh	1932-34	21	15	2	1				
Minto Scott	1998-2002	44+7		2		4	2		
Mitchell Paul	1993-94	+1							
Moncur John	1994-2002	131+44	6	7+1	1	13+1		5+1	
Moore Brian	1954-56	9	1						
Moore Bobby	1958-73	543+1	24	36		49	3	13	
Moore Ian	1997-98	+1			6				
Moore Billy	1922-28	181	42	21					
Morgan Nicky	1978-82	14+7	2			1			
Morley Trevor	1989-94	159+19	57	14+5	7	10+1	5	1+2	

Player	Played	Lge	Gls	FAC	Gls	LC	Gls	Euro	Gls	PO	Gls
Moroney Tommy	1947-52	148	8	3							
Morris Bob	1919-20	3									
Morton John	1931-38	258	54	17	3						
Moyes Jim	1919-20	2	1								
Mullins Hayden	2003-	115+14	3	13+1	3	4					6
Murray Frank	1919-20	2									
Musgrave Joe	1930-35	36	1	4	1						
Musgrove Malcolm	1953-62	283	84	13	2	5	3				
Neary Frank	1946-47	17	15								
Neighbour Jimmy	1979-82	66+7	5	6+1		11+1	1	4			
Neill Lucas	2006-	11		1							
Nelson Andy	1955-58	15	1								
Nelson Bill	1954-55	2									
Neville Billy	1957-58	3									
Newell Mike	1996-97	6+1									
Newman Mick	1956-57	7	2					+1			
Newton Adam	1999-2000	+2									
Newton Shaun	2004-07	19+21	1	2+2		1+1				2+1	
Noble David	2003-04	+3				1				+3	
Noble Mark	2004-	24+4	2	4	1	1+2					
Norrington Cyril	1927-28	27	6								
Norris Fred	1928-32	65	1								
Nowland Adam	2003-05	5+10				2					
Obeney Harry	1956-60	25	12	2							

Player	Years									
O'Farrell Frank	1950-56	197	6	13	1	+1				
Omoyinmi Manny	1996-98	1+8	2	1+1		1				
Orhan Yilmaz	1975-76	6+2								
Orr Neil	1981-87	133+13	4	10+1		14+4	1			
Otulakowski Anton	1976-77	10+7								
Paddon Graham	1973-76	115	11	11		11	2	9		
Palmer James	1919-20	13	1							
Pantsill John	2006-	3+2		+1		1				
Parker Derek	1946-56	199	9	8						
Parker Reg	1935-36	2								
Parkes Phil	1978-89	344		34		52		6		
Parks Tony	1991-92	6		3						
Parris George	1984-92	211+28	12	21	4	27+3	1			
Parsons Eric	1946-50	145	34	6	1					
Payne Joe	1946-47	10	6	1						
Payne John	1926-28	4	1							
Pearce Ian	1997-2002	135+7	9	10+1	1	8		1+1		E
Pearce Stuart	1999-2000	42	2	4	1	4				
Pearson Stuart	1979-81	28+6	6	8+2	2	3+2	1	+1		
Petchey George	1952-53	2								
Peters Martin	1961-69	302	81	16	5	31	10	15	2	4
Phillips Wilf	1931-32	21	3	2						
Phipps Cecil	1919-20	1								
Pike Geoff	1975-86	275+16	32	29+2	5	38+1	3	6		E
Pollard Walter	1929-32	37	3	6	2					

Player	Played	Lge	Gls	FAC	Gls	LC	Gls	Euro	Gls	PO	Gls
Porfirio Hugo	1996-97	15+8	2	1+1	1	2	1				3
Potts Steve	1984-2000	362+37	1	41+1		39+3		7+1			
Powell Chris	2004-05	35+1		3							
Powell Darren	2004-05	5	1								
Presland Eddie	1964-65	6	1								
Proctor Norman	1923-24	7	1								
Proudlock George	1938-47	18	5								
Puddefoot Syd	1919-32	125	67	8	5						
Pyke Malcolm	1956-57	17		2							
Quashie Nigel	2006-	7		1							
Quinn Jimmy	1989-90	34+13	19	4+2	2	3	1				
Quinn Wayne	2003-04	22		2+1		2					
Radford John	1976-77	28		1		1					
Raducioiu Florin	1996-97	6+5	2				1				
Rebrov Sergei	2004-05	12+14	1	1+1		2+1	1			+1	
Redknapp Harry	1965-71	146+3	7	7+1		17+1	1	2			
Reid Kyle	2005-	1+1				1					
Reo-Coker Nigel	2003-07	113+7	11	9+1		4				3+3	
Repka Tomas	2001-06	164		9+1		8				6	
Rhodes Brian	1957-62	61		2		3					
Richards Dick	1922-23	43	5	10	1						
Richardson Frank	1923-24	10	2	1							
Rieper Marc	1994-97	83+7	5	4		6+1					
Robinson Bill	1948-51	101	60	4	1						

Name	Years									
Robinson Les	1920-24	19	2							
Roberts Viv	1919-20	1								
Roberts Bill	1937-38	1								
Robson Bryan	1970-78	227	94	12	4	15	6	9	4	1 / 3
Robson George	1927-30	17	2	1	1	7	1			
Robson Keith	1974-76	65+3	13	3	1	2	1			
Robson Mark	1992-93	42+5	8	2	1	8	1			
Robson Stewart	1986-90	68+1	4	6			1			
Robson Bill	1933-34	3								
Rosenior Leroy	1987-91	44+9	15	4+1	2	7	2			
Rowland Keith	1993-97	63+17	1	5+1		3+2		5+1		
Ruddock Neil	1998-99	39+3	2	3		3+1		5+1		
Rush Matthew	1990-94	29+19	5			4				
Ruffell Jimmy	1921-36	505	159	43	7					
Rutherford Jack	1933-34	33		2						
Sadler George	1946-47	1								
Scaloni Lionel	2005-06	13		3+1						
Schemmel Seb	2000-02	60+3	1	7		2+1	3			
Scott Tony	1959-65	83	16	7		7	1	7		
Sealey Alan	1960-66	107	22	8		6	1			
Sealey Les	1995-96	2+2								
Sexton Dave	1952-55	74	27	3	2					1+2
Shea Danny	1920-21	16	1							
Shearing Peter	1960-61	6								
Sheringham Teddy	2004-07	45+31	28	3+4	2	1+2		+1		

Player	Played	Lge	Gls	FAC	Gls	LC	Gls	Euro	Gls	PO	Gls
Shone Danny	1928-29	12	5								
Simmons Jim	1920-21	27	1								
Simpson Peter	1935-36	32	12	4							
Sinclair Trevor	1997-2002	175+2	37	8	8	9+1					
Sissons John	1962-69	210+3	37	18		21	5	10			
Slater Robbie	1995-96	18+7	2	1		3	2	13			
Slater Stuart	1987-91	134+7	11	16	3	16+1					
Smailes Matt	1928-29	7		3							
Small Mike	1991-92	42+7	13	4+1	1	4+1	4				
Small Sam	1936-47	108	40	10							
Smillie Andy	1958-60	20	3	3							
Smith David	1919-20	1	1								
Smith Harry	1927-28	1									
Smith John	1956-59	125	20	5	2						
Smith Mark	1979-80	1				1					
Smith Roy	1955-56	6	1		1						
Smith Steve	1919-21	27	1	4							
Smith William	1927-28	2									
Smithurst Edgar	1919-20	3									
Sofiane Youseff	2003-04	+1		1+1		1					
Soma Rangvald	2000-01	3+4	1	1							
Song Rigobert	2000-01	23+1		2		2					
Southren Tommy	1950-53	64	3								
Speedie David	1992-93	11	4	2							

Player	Years							
Spector Jonathan	2006-	17+8		1+1				1
Smicek Pavel	2003-04	2+1						
Standen Jim	1962-67	178		20		23		14
Stanley Tom	1919-20	1						
Stephens Bill	1947-48	22	6	2	1	6		
Stephenson Alan	1967-71	106+2		4	1	14		
Stewart Ray	1979-90	344+1	62	35+1	7	44	14	6
Stimac Igor	1999-2000	43	1	2		5		2
Stockdale Robbie	2003-04	5+2		1		1		
Stokes Tony	2005-					+1		
StPier Wally	1929-32	24						
Strodder Gary	1986-89	59+6	2	4+2		8		6+1
Stroud Roy	1951-56	13	4			5	1	
Suckling Perry	1989-90	6				1		
Suker Davor	2000-01	7+4	2			1+1	1	
Swindlehurst Dave	1982-84	52+9	16	4+1	1	5		9
Taricco Mauricio	2004-05	1						
Tate Isaac	1927-28	14						
Taylor Alan	1974-78	88+10	25	7+1	6	8	2	6+1
Taylor George	1946-55	115	3	3				9
Taylor Tommy	1970-78	340	8	21		26		9
Terrier David	1997-98	+1						
Tevez Carlos	2006-	19+7	7	1				2
Thirlaway Bill	1921-23	36	2	3				
Thomas Mitchell	1991-92	37+1	3	4		5		

Player	Played	Lge	Gls	FAC	Gls	LC	Gls	Euro	Gls	PO	Gls
Thorpe Percy	1933-34	3									
Thinen Hannu	2000-01	5+3									
Tindall Ron	1961-62	13	3								
Tippett Tommy	1933-35	27	10								
Tirrell Alf	1919-20	1									
Todorov Svetoslav	2000-01	4+10	1	+2	1	1					
Tonner Arthur	1935-36	1									
Travis Don	1946-47	5									
Tresadern Jack	1919-24	144	5	16							
Tucker Ken	1947-56	83	31	10							
Turner Charles	1937-38	11									
Turner Cyril	1919-21	7	1								
Tyler Dudley	1972-73	29	1	2		3					
Unsworth Dave	1997-98	32	2	4		5					
Upson Matthew	2006-	2									
VanDer Elst Francois	1981-82	61+1	14	2	2	5+1	3				
Wade Don	1947-49	36	5	4							
Wade Reg	1929-31	32		1							
Wade Bill	1929-31	16									
Walford Steve	1983-86	114+1	2	14		16+1	2				
Walker Albert	1932-37	162		12							
Walker Charlie	1936-38	110		8							
Walker Dick	1934-52	292	2	19		3					
Walker james	2004-	13		1							3

Player	Years	Apps	Gls	FA App	FA Gl	LC App	LC Gl
Wallbanks Fred	1934-35			1			
Wanchope Paulo	1999-2000	33+2	12	+1		2	
Ward Elliott	2004-06	13+2				3	
Ward Mark	1985-89	163+2	12	17		20+1	
Watson George	1932-34	33		5			
Watson Mark	1995-96	+1					
Watson Vic	1920-34	462	298	43	28		
Waugh William	1921-22	6		1			
Weale Bobby	1925-26	3					
Weare Jack	1936-37	57		2			
Webster Joe	1919-20	2		2			
Webster Simon	1994-95	+5		1		2+1	
Weldon Tony	1931-32	20	3	1			
Whitbread Adrian	1994-95	3+7		1		2+1	
Whitton Steve	1983-84	35+4	6			6	
Williams Gavin	2004-05	7+3	1			1	
Williams Harry	1951-52	5	1				
Williams Rod	1937-38	9					
Williams Billy	1921-26	35	5				
Williamson Danny	1993-96	47+4				+2	
Wilson Arthur	1932-33	29					
Wilson Ron	1946-47	3					
Winterburn Nigel	2000-02	78+4	1			3+1	
Wood Jacky	1937-48	58	13	4			
Wood Jimmy	1929-34	63	14	1			

Player	Played	Lge	Gls	FAC	Gls	LC	Gls	Euro	Gls	PO	Gls
Woodards Dan	1919-20	16									
Woodburn John	1919-20	4									
Woodgate Terry	1928-52	259	48	16	4						
Woodley Derek	1959-61	12	3			1					
Wooler Alan	1973-75	3+1		1		4					
Woosnam Phil	1958-62	138	26	5			1				
Wragg Doug	1955-59	16									
Wright George	1951-57	161		9							
Wright Ian	1998-99	20+2	9	1		2		+1			
Wright Ken	1946-49	51	20	1							
Wyllie Bob	1956-57	13		2							
Yeomanson Jack	1947-50	106	1	5	5						
Yews Tommy	1923-32	332	46	29							
Young Jack	1919-25	124	3	14							
Young Len	1933-37	12									
Zamora Bobby	2003-	74+43	29	3+6	2	4	4	1+1		6	4